T0277723

Praise for AJ Richichi and

HOURLY

Hourly is simply required reading for any leader or manager trying to build a better team or working to improve the performance of the team they have in their stores, trucks, warehouses, or service centers. In contrast to the nearly endless number of books focused on the "top of the house," *Hourly* drills down to the front lines and the back rooms that power the enterprise and form the foundation of nearly every successful business.

While working at home during the pandemic, my son asked me after a few months why I spent so much time talking about, worrying about, and trying to retain and develop our 600 drivers who were still on the road every day. I replied that without our hourly workers still putting it on the line in our stores, and our drivers out delivering our products to customers, we wouldn't have a business. But I also realized that even to a middle school kid, our hourly workforce seemed invisible.

AJ brings this often-invisible workforce into highly visible focus. Loaded with real-life examples and actionable insights,

Hourly can help us all recruit, retain, and develop those team members who ring the register and take care of customers every hour of every day.

DOUG HAUGH

Chief Commercial Officer, Vertex Energy

How can such an essential and massive workforce, who form the backbone of the US economy, be so misunderstood and invisible? Yet it is. AJ Richichi shares why, how it can change for the better, and how his solutions can lift the veil on this critical employee base. All companies with an hourly workforce owe AJ a huge thanks for the insights contained in *Hourly*.

LAURA VARN

Vice President, People & Culture and Communications, Parkland

Hourly is THE Manifesto for leading, inspiring, and retaining your hourly workforce!

BEN FANNING

Host of *Lead the Team* (Top 2% Globally Ranked Podcast)

AJ Richichi's *Hourly* is a "must-read" book for anyone looking to gain a deep and unique insight into the world of hourly workers. The author reminds us of the value of these workers and their importance in our lives as customers and business practitioners. Mr. Richichi's book speaks to the crisis that is before us in the hiring and retention of these essential workers. He recognizes that equitable compensation, a meaningful work life, and caring organizations must be integral components of any solution.

The real-life, concrete examples presented in *Hourly* are truly compelling, providing a path forward for businesses. Brand leaders such as Panda Restaurant Group and Sweetgreen are empowering their employees and engaging them in the formulation of policies. I found myself both inspired by these brands and hopeful that the vision of a more inclusive economy was possible.

A book like *Hourly* is long overdue and should be at the top of the reading list for anyone who cares about the future of our workforce.

NATALIE BLACHER

former Vice President of Strategic Planning, Burger King;

former CMO, McAlister's Deli

HOURLY

Empowering
the Invisible Workforce
for Shared Success

HOURLY

AJ **Richichi**
Founder and CEO, Sprockets

Foreword by
Natalie Rothman
Chief People Officer,
Inspire Brands

Forbes | Books

Published by Forbes Books, Charleston, South Carolina.
An imprint of Advantage Media Group.

Forbes Books is a registered trademark, and the Forbes Books colophon is a trademark of Forbes Media, LLC.

Printed in the United States of America.

10 9 8 7 6 5 4 3 2 1

ISBN: 979-8-88750-561-9 (Hardcover)
ISBN: 979-8-88750-562-6 (eBook)

Library of Congress Control Number: 2024904914

Cover and layout design by Matthew Morse.

This custom publication is intended to provide accurate information and the opinions of the author in regard to the subject matter covered. It is sold with the understanding that the publisher, Forbes Books, is not engaged in rendering legal, financial, or professional services of any kind. If legal advice or other expert assistance is required, the reader is advised to seek the services of a competent professional.

Since 1917, Forbes has remained steadfast in its mission to serve as the defining voice of entrepreneurial capitalism. Forbes Books, launched in 2016 through a partnership with Advantage Media, furthers that aim by helping business and thought leaders bring their stories, passion, and knowledge to the forefront in custom books. Opinions expressed by Forbes Books authors are their own. To be considered for publication, please visit **books.Forbes.com**.

To the invisible workers who brought this book to life:

Those who printed our copies,

Those who packed the boxes,

Those who kept us caffeinated,

And so much more.

We see you.

Contents

About the Author

AJ Richichi: Innovator, Leader, and Community Advocate

In the dynamic world of technology and innovation, AJ Richichi stands out as a visionary leader with a deep commitment to industry excellence and community engagement. Born and raised in the vibrant state of New York, AJ's journey from his early years to becoming the CEO and founder of Sprockets is marked by a passion for technology, a dedication to community service, and a relentless pursuit of excellence.

During his teenage years, AJ demonstrated a keen interest in public service, working in the US Senate on Capitol Hill. This early exposure to the intricacies of policymaking ignited a spark within him, setting the stage for a career that seamlessly blended technology and community impact.

AJ's professional journey is punctuated by numerous accolades that attest to his outstanding contributions. He earned recognition as one of the "Best and Brightest Under 35" in South Carolina, acknowledging his leadership and impact on the tech landscape. His role as the Technology Executive of the Year in Upstate New York further solidified his reputation as a trailblazer in the industry. The "40 under

40" honor in Upstate New York is a testament to AJ's multifaceted influence, extending beyond his role as a technology executive.

Beyond his professional pursuits, AJ Richichi is deeply committed to giving back to the community. Serving as the cochair of Charleston Open Source and founder of DisruptHR Greenville, he actively contributes to the technology community, fostering collaboration and innovation. AJ is also a valued member of the Tech Advisory Committee at SC Codes, where he plays a crucial role in shaping the technological landscape in South Carolina. As a mentor and judge at the Citadel and College of Charleston, AJ invests time and expertise in guiding the next generation of tech enthusiasts.

Currently, AJ is at the helm of Sprockets, a technology company he founded. Sprockets is dedicated to equitably connecting millions of hourly workers with some of the world's most recognizable brands. Under AJ's leadership, Sprockets has become a pioneer in the tech industry, facilitating meaningful connections between workers and brands.

On a personal note, AJ is happily married to his high school sweetheart, Jordan, and together they are raising two children. They call Daniel Island, South Carolina, home, where AJ finds joy in spending time with his family, particularly at the beach.

AJ Richichi's journey embodies the essence of a modern leader—driven, compassionate, and dedicated to creating a tech-driven future that benefits all.

Foreword

Natalie Rothman: Chief People Officer of Inspire Brands

Growing up, I never aspired exactly to be a Chief People Officer, but I was raised in a family that showed me the profound impact, through even the smallest of actions, that you can have on someone else's life. My father was a neurosurgeon for over 50 years and taught me that when you take the Hippocratic Oath as a doctor, you have a duty to take care of every patient, and he spent his life dedicated to healing others. My brother Philip followed in our father's footsteps and found his calling as a paramedic and a Captain in the Fire Rescue Department of Broward County, Florida. He, too, developed a passion for helping others, even if it meant risking his own life.

While I took a different career path than my family, I knew I wanted to do something where I could have a positive impact on people and learn more about business. Some of my favorite business mentors taught me the importance of spending time where the work actually gets done with the most important people in our business — frontline team members — or, as AJ Richichi refers to them in his new book, the Invisible Workforce. Throughout my career, I've believed in the importance of seeing the workplace through the eyes of the hourly team member. At PepsiCo, I delivered cases of products on route rides and merchandised shelves in stores. At Advance Auto Parts, I put away car parts in our distribution centers, and now, in my role at Inspire Brands, I have worked in restaurants, making great food for our guests to enjoy.

I have also observed my mentors personally connecting with our hourly team members and learning more about their families and what they liked about working with us. One mentor would take notes on his iPad with everyone's name and a suggestion on what they would change if they could. He never forgot a name and made everyone he spoke with feel special. These field visits working side by side with frontline team members made me appreciate how challenging their job could be, as well as gave me great ideas on how to simplify work, reduce team member turnover, and ultimately improve business results.

My work experiences culminated in me joining Inspire, the second-largest restaurant company in the United States, as the Chief People Officer in May 2023. Inspire and its franchise organizations employ more than 675,000 team members, most of whom are at the hourly level. I was attracted to the company because of its strong culture, capable management team, and focus on people at every level. The best part about my role is when a frontline team member tells us that they feel "seen" after receiving recognition for doing their job well or a promotion to a new role.

Hourly: Empowering the Invisible Workforce for Shared Success is a great read for employers who seek to unlock the full potential of their hourly workforce. This book offers great suggestions on how to hire the best people for your culture and how to leverage technology to automate work so managers and Human Resources professionals can spend more time coaching and developing their teams. It's earned its place as a mainstay in my library as the book's lessons are meaningful, actionable, and relevant.

Introduction

Nearly ten years ago, I met with a billionaire at his penthouse in New York City. At the time, I was selling software that used personality modeling to predict success in professional athletes. In short, we were helping teams determine which athletes fit their organization's culture and which did not—something this billionaire desperately needed to support his teams after a decade of bad draft picks.

I approached the meeting much as I'd approached meetings in the past. I woke up in my hotel room, walked downstairs for a cityscape run, broke for coffee, and then waited anxiously in the meeting lobby while listening to my favorite pump-up songs.

This billionaire wasn't the type to go into the office. He preferred to manage his vast empire from an outdated Blackberry, fax machine, and legal notepad—all from the comfort of his fifty-million-dollar penthouse. He was also the type of guy to look at me, a teenage kid in an Ivy League blazer, and tell me to take a hike without remorse.

I knew I had a two-minute window to either earn an hour or the door.

My strategy in sales is to get personal as quickly as possible. That's the millennial in me. I'm known to share an embarrassing story or flash a glimpse of my kids to break awkwardness in the sales process. The chances of me walking in and convincing this walking BS detector that the technology I originally designed in high school would win him a professional championship were very low. I needed something special.

In my research, I learned that his first business was a small restaurant that tanked in the 1980s. It was his only failed business in a career of unbelievable prosperity and success. I called every person in the town where his restaurant was located until I found an ex-employee named Danny. For a $100 gift card, this person spilled their guts. Old stories, nicknames, you name it. What stood out in that conversation was Danny's simultaneous lack of surprise for the billionaire's lifelong success and the restaurant's failure.

"When he [the billionaire] took over," Danny said, "it was as if he was leading from a business management seminar. He set up KPIs and explained in fine detail the importance of unit economics, but he never learned any of our names. The man-child even printed out a quote from some fancy philosophy book during the Roman Empire. He treated us like cogs and expected robotic results, but even I knew that wouldn't work."

Admittedly, the importance of this story didn't register with me at the time. Out of all the lessons to digest, I memorized an abstract quote from Marcus Aurelius to reference as if we were of similar minds and interests in the upcoming conversation with the billionaire. During our exchange, I managed to slip in a "You know, what hurts the bee hurts the storm." I smiled ear to ear, waiting for an affirmative head nod when all I received was an eye roll and "I have a hard stop in ten minutes."

With one last shot and not enough time to properly pitch my company's entire suite of products, I came clean about researching his past and told him that Danny wanted me to say hi. I took my MacBook off the marble countertop, collected the freshly printed presentations, thanked him for his time, and shook his hand while looking down at my shoes. When I turned my back to him, I remember taking a deep breath, closing my eyes in anguish, and taking the first step toward the en-suite elevator.

As soon as my second foot hit the floor, I heard him say words that changed my life forever.

"So, you want to know, don't you?"

"Know what, sir?"

"How on earth I tanked a restaurant and then built this." His hands spread wide as if measuring a marlin he caught off his 130-foot yacht.

I smiled in complete disbelief and with no air in my lungs. Without thinking, words fell from my mouth. It was do or die. "I know why."

"OK, kid. I'll bite. Why?"

"You didn't see your workers."

Silence.

A part of me wanted to apologize instantly, and the other part wanted to curl up in a ball right on his Italian-stained floor, but I stood there staring at him through the discomfort.

For the first time in the meeting, he smiled. My sweaty palms regripped my bag that was quickly feeling heavier and heavier. The billionaire walked to the refrigerator, grabbed a water bottle, and put it in front of me.

"Stay for a few more minutes. Let me tell you a story."

The word "fate" gives me the ick. However, even in that moment I started to feel a new energy. A new magic in that room. There was something about this topic that interested this billionaire enough to drop everything. An intrigue. An obsession. I had stumbled upon something divine to him.

"Minutes" quickly turned into an entire day.

Almost cathartically, this billionaire shared the restaurant's story from start to finish and why he picked that particular location. He shared how he scraped enough money together to fix the fryer right before the Super Bowl and the music he'd play to encourage subconscious spending. Most of all, he lamented about his biggest mistake: how he managed the "Dannys." He explained that at such a young age, he'd focused all his energy on the voice of the customer and completely neglected the people who served them.

"With problems constantly coming up to solve, I made an age-old mistake that my responsibility to the Dannys was on Friday afternoons when payroll was processed. That's it." He credited the business's failure to this mindset. He couldn't keep the restaurant staffed. Customers felt the team's dissatisfaction, and when things got hard, he didn't have a team that had his back. He lost everything.

For the rest of his life and future businesses, he explained that he corrected and, at times, over-incentivized his teams. He met each employee, even when he had thousands, in their first week. He paid well. He provided top-of-the-line benefits. He stopped treating people like numbers. "Pay, perks, that's all great. But the workforce, above all, needs to feel *seen*."

During this conversation, he kept using the phrase "Invisible Workforce" to describe his hourly workers. It struck me. At the time, it felt harsh. I thought he was being hyperbolic, but this wasn't the type of person to use words recklessly or unintentionally, especially ones of such significance.

As the conversation proceeded and I missed my flight because we were four hours over our scheduled time, a central message emerged. He felt that seeing the invisible workforce—the Dannys—was his competitive advantage. While his peers struggled throughout the years, he credited his success to learning this lesson early in his career and relentlessly committing to amazing his workers regardless if they were cleaning the floors or running his board meetings. Most importantly, this concept scaled. It allowed him to flourish in several industries, economies, and every sized business.

After our second meal together that day, he walked me to the elevator.

As the doors were closing, he said one last thing to me:

"Say hi to Danny for me."

There are few moments in life that shift your perspective. The day you marry your best friend. The first time you hold your child. The day you learn the truth about Santa. For me, this was one of those days.

As I stepped off the elevator, for the first time, I saw them: the invisible workforce. I noticed the red tie on the doorman. I saw the beads of sweat on the street sweeper's face. I stood and watched the window washers on the adjourning skyscraper. A woman with beautiful tattoos was playing the piano at the corner bar. The bartender who handed her some water had red hair. On the trip home, I thought about how many invisible workers needed to work together for my safe flight. The taxi driver to the airport. The person who printed my ticket. The employee that took my carry-on. Security. People assisting the elderly. Workers at the gate. The guys with the lightsaber things directing traffic. Attendants handing me pretzels and making sure my seat was buckled.

"Did these people feel seen?"

"Did they have the tools to be successful?"

"How could companies better serve them?"

In under twenty-four hours, I pivoted my company and life's focus to find the answers to these questions. This book covers the lessons I've learned on the journey through conversations with the world's largest employers, venture capitalists, economists, technology providers, and millions of people in the hourly workforce.

CHAPTER 1

The Misunderstood Majority

As humans, we have a tendency to go about our lives with "blinders" on that keep us oblivious to anything—or anyone—that don't seem directly related to the tasks at hand each day. I had these blinders on when preparing for my meeting with that billionaire. I didn't pay much attention to the barista who made my coffee, the officer directing traffic so I could go for my morning run safely, or the executive assistant who kindly offered me the glass of water I gulped down while anxiously waiting in the lobby. The only thing that ran through my mind that morning was a slideshow of situations I needed to be ready for in my big meeting. Many of us have this goal-driven, no-time-for-distractions type of mindset that make us blind to those who actually make such significant contributions in helping us accomplish our goals. Luckily, I had that moment of realization that allowed me to truly see the often-overlooked workers all around me, understand the impact they have, and dedicate my life to solving the widescale problems they face. I hope this book serves as a similar moment of realization as we shine a light on the invisible workforce. It's time to remove the blinders and see the forest for the trees—while appreciating the trees along the way.

Meet Marco.

He lives in a 900-square-foot apartment with his wife and two children. He drives a 2007 Nissan Sentra that doesn't start if the temperature dips below 30 degrees. He has $924.81 in his bank account, $15,361 in credit card debt, and $12,458 in medical bills. He doesn't have a credit score but somehow owes a college $18,999 for classes he took twenty years ago. Still, he uses private loans to cover rent each month with a 27 percent interest rate.

Marco isn't unemployed. He works fifty hours a week as a call center representative, then picks up odd jobs to help make ends meet. Marco is someone you'd likely start a GoFundMe page for if his dog got sick.

When you look at Marco's life, you may think to yourself, "What did he do to put himself in this situation?" or "Wow, Marco must have had some bad luck."

However, Marco's story is unfortunately common. He has more money than the average hourly worker. He has less debt, fewer bills, and a relatively small college loan debt compared to his peers. Marco is living and breathing in a class that I call "the invisible majority" of America, the nearly 80,000,000 people that punch a time clock at work.

People like Marco, those in the hourly workforce, power our economy, with few people actually noticing them. They're the ones who make our coffee. They cook our breakfast sandwiches. They pump our gas. They mop the floors and clean the bathrooms. They care for our loved ones and manage our frustration in call centers. They complete these and other tasks that are often taken for granted.

Meet the Hourly Workforce

The hourly workforce is often misunderstood, and it's important to establish and understand the lives of these people before making any judgments or suggestions.

Almost 56 percent of the country's workforce is hourly, or 78.7 million people. That's more total people than an entire country such as England, France, or Italy. More people work for hourly wages in America than in Denmark, Finland, New Zealand, Ireland, Costa Rica, Portugal, Greece, Netherlands, Puerto Rico, and Singapore combined.

A common misunderstanding is that those who clock in and clock out are younger high school kids working part-time jobs to save for college, but that's simply untrue. Only 20 percent of this population is under the age of twenty-six. The two largest cohorts in the hourly workforce are millennials and Gen Xers, with the percentage of baby boomers quickly increasing in recent years. As inflation rises and the labor market shrinks for talent, older Americans have returned to the workforce.

Eighty-five percent of hourly workers have a high school diploma or GED. Sixty-five percent pursued college, but only 14 percent of hourly workers have earned a bachelor's degree or higher. This is significantly lower than salaried workers and the average American. In fact, nearly 40 percent of Americans have a bachelor's degree today, or 2.5× more than the hourly workforce.[1]

Even for those who get college degrees, it can take a long time to secure their ideal salaried jobs after graduation—something that a lot of people can't wait for, especially when they have spouses and children to support. So they jump into an hourly job temporarily until they find something better. Or, many of them started out in the hourly workforce after high school and worked their butts off to get a degree with night classes. Either way, it's not ideal, and it typically results in student loan debt that many of them can't afford.

Despite some hourly positions with strong pay and opportunities, the vast majority of hourly workers are under-resourced. Forty-eight percent of hourly workers in the United States don't have a single cent in emergency savings (up 7 percent YoY).[2] Credit card debt across America is at an all-time high, surpassing $1,000,000,000,000. That's a lot of zeroes, and it's getting bigger every quarter. The average consumer owes over $6,000 in credit card debt, up 10+ percent YoY. With interest rates climbing, this grows each month. In fact, the average credit card interest rate on these accounts assessed interest of, on average, 22.77 percent, according to the Federal Reserve in 2023. Credit card debt, especially in the hourly workforce, does not improve over time. It gets worse. While the average person in their twenties has $2,900 in debt, that number continues to increase year after year: $5,800 in your thirties, $7,600 in your forties.

1   US Bureau of Labor Statistics, "Characteristics of Minimum Wage Workers, 2021," January 7, 2022, https://www.bls.gov/opub/reports/minimum-wage/2022/home.htm#:~:text=Education.,a%20bachelor's%20degree%20and%20higher.

2   Alain Sherter, "48% of Hourly Workers in the U.S. Don't Have a Single Cent in Emergency Savings," CBS News, July 20, 2022, https://www.cbsnews.com/news/saving-money-inflation-hourly-worker-minimum-wage/.

Lack of financial opportunities and access to financial literacy education takes its toll on this group. According to the Consumer Financial Protection Bureau, twenty-six million US adults have no credit history with the three national credit bureaus: TransUnion, Experian, and Equifax. As a result, they have no credit scores.[3] This restricts their ability to open any line of credit, apply for housing, get proper medical care, buy a cell phone, and countless other things. Buying a car, applying for a business loan, and earning stomachable interest rates are not possibilities for this group. So, when they incur hardship, their holes are dug deeper. In many ways, they must fight twice as hard as others to get to the same playing field.

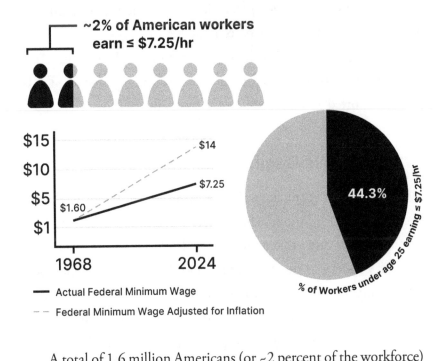

~2% of American workers earn ≤ $7.25/hr

$15
$10
$5
$1
$14
$7.25
$1.60
1968   2024

— Actual Federal Minimum Wage
– – Federal Minimum Wage Adjusted for Inflation

44.3%

earning ≤ $7.25/hr

% of Workers under age 25

A total of 1.6 million Americans (or ~2 percent of the workforce) earn less or equal to the federal minimum wage of $7.25 an hour. This

3   National Credit Union Administration, "Serving the Credit Invisible," accessed February 6, 2024, https://ncua.gov/files/publications/serving-credit-invisibles.pdf.

is heavier on younger workers, with 44.3 percent of workers under the age of twenty-five earning that figure. The federal minimum wage has not changed in over fifteen years. It is not adjusted for inflation. In 1968, minimum wage was $1.60. When adjusted for inflation, that same earning would be around $14 today, or 93 percent more than the current number.

Eighteen states have maintained the federal minimum wage, while the others have increased it across the state. California, Washington DC, Massachusetts, and Washington state have more than doubled their minimum wage laws in the past ten years. Women make less than men, even in the hourly workforce. Sixty-two percent of minimum wage workers are females, 28 percent of minimum wage workers are parents, and 48 percent are married.

Broadly speaking, hourly workers are in the thick of it. While they service salaried workers and power the economy, they need to be more supported and noticed.

Where Do We Begin?

When we talk with companies about humanizing the hourly workforce, there's a tendency to think that it starts with their worker's first day on the job. However, that's not the case. It starts earlier. Much earlier.

Let's zoom out our perspective and think bigger. Think about what someone must go through prior to employment—a hiring process that's stressful, time-consuming, and often riddled with bias. Job seekers typically must go through this frustrating process numerous times at different businesses before actually securing an opportunity. So, while their first day is an important aspect to analyze when looking into how to humanize the hourly workforce, let's start at where they begin their journey: the job hunt and subsequent steps involved in screening and selection.

Say Marco is looking for a new job. Where does he get the first impression of a potential employer? Often, it's an unpleasant conversation with a manager who may be too overworked and exhausted to guide him through the application process. Sure, you might say his first impression could be the "careers" or "about us" pages on the company's website if he does a search online, but aren't so many of those pages basically the same?

This company may share an uplifting story of how they value diversity, community, and collaboration, but Marco's actual first experience at the business is anything but uplifting. Again, the manager may not even realize the impression he gave Marco—especially if he is trying to keep the lights on at an understaffed business. The manager is probably working double shifts and covering additional tasks that he normally wouldn't have to do. So even though this conversation with a job seeker could help solve their staffing issues, it's the exact thing that could deter a potentially great hire.

Instead of assuming Marco went directly to the place of business to complete a paper application by hand, let's think about the scenario in which he does a job search online. In this case, he doesn't have any particular company in mind. He's just looking for any business nearby that's hiring for an entry-level position he could fill. He navigates to a job board, sets his parameters, and types "crew member" in the search bar. Dozens of listings populate on his screen. He starts clicking through the options, subconsciously eliminating them one by one. Job description too long. Next. Description too hard to read. Next. Too many typos. Next. No mention of pay rate. Next. Doesn't explain the role clearly. Next. Finally, he just starts skimming job titles and clicking "Apply" to a dozen or so listings.

Hold on a second. At this point, you may be asking why on earth he'd move through this process so aggressively. With turnover rates at astronomical levels in the hourly workforce, Marco will likely leave or get terminated from this job within a few months—maybe less. Unlike salaried workers, hourly workers have been conditioned to have more jobs, so they are not romanticized by the hiring process or selective in their choices. They've experienced so much rejection, frustration, and toxicity in various work environments that they've simply accepted the expectation that they will only work somewhere for a short time before having to go through this process all over again. It could be a dozen times in a year.

It's also important to note that as Marco quickly sifted through the job listings online and skipped them for one reason or another, they could've been telling him something about each company that would contribute to his initial opinions of the companies. The one with the job description that was too long? One could assume the hiring process will also be lengthy and time-consuming. He needs a job ASAP. The job description that was too hard to read? He might assume upper management doesn't really know their frontline workers or how they talk about hourly jobs. The job description with all those typos? It screams, "They clearly rushed through this and didn't care enough to put in the effort." They might similarly not care much about treating their workers well. Then, we come to the listing that doesn't list a pay rate. It could be because they aren't offering much and don't want to deter applicants. Onto the next one. It didn't explain the role well enough. That can be a huge pet peeve for job seekers and a particularly frustrating problem for those who eventually get the job after a long hiring process only to realize the position is nothing like they expected it to be. Basically, all of these examples get the job experience off to a negative start.

Now, what's next for Marco?

...

Waiting.

It can be an enormous frustration for job seekers when they submit an application and then have to wait days or weeks to get a simple response. People would rather get a reply telling them the manager, unfortunately, went with another candidate than get nothing at all. Even if hiring managers don't intend for it to come off this way, it can feel like they don't respect the individuals they ignore. And good luck getting that person to apply again for any future opportunities you need to fill at your company. While they should try not to take it personally since busy managers probably just didn't have time and didn't respond to dozens of other applicants, it can still send a negative message about how your company values its workforce.

Now, let's get into everyone's favorite part: the interview process. This stage can make or break the candidate's experience, making someone feel valued or less than others. Say Marco's car didn't start that morning, and he had to run to the bus stop to make it to the interview on time. No time for coffee or breakfast. This is the single most important aspect of his day. Heck, maybe his week or beyond, as he thinks about the bills this job opportunity could help him pay. Huffing and puffing still from running to the bus, he makes it to his interview location and steps through the doors.

"Can I help you?"

"Yes, I'm here for my interview with Mike, the manager here."

"Hmm. OK, hold on. I'll go get him... Yeah, he said he's in the middle of something and is going to be about fifteen minutes late. You can have a seat over there while you wait."

Shocked and somewhat dejected, Marco grabs a chair and waits. He went through all this trouble to make it to his interview on time, but the manager will be late after all. It's OK, he reassures himself by thinking it must be something important.

About twenty-five minutes later, Mike emerges from the back office. "Sorry, I was on the phone with my wife."

Not a great start.

Still, maybe it was important. Marco puts his game face on with a strong smile and handshake. The interview goes on for a good hour, with Mike mostly just reading through the résumé word for word that Marco submitted weeks ago. "Sorry, I haven't actually had a chance to look this over."

One more handshake, smile, and a "We'll be in touch" before Marco heads back out to the bus stop. Fingers crossed, that went well, although it sure didn't feel like it.

He keeps thinking about it during the bus ride to his current job. *He couldn't have been on time for the interview with me? He didn't even care to read my résumé ahead of time? Did he ask any meaningful questions about me, my career goals, and why I wanted to work there?*

He hears the sound of the brakes and gets off the bus once again to go to work, only to step inside and immediately hear, "Why are you late again?"

Another day as an hourly worker.

What's the next step? Oh, right. The next step in the process is...

...

Waiting. Again. Often with no response at all if they hired someone else.

Again, I can't emphasize enough that it's not necessarily the manager's fault since so many managers are understaffed and overworked these days. And, of course, this is a fictional representation—although close to what hourly workers deal with on a regular basis.

Key Takeaways

So, we've ventured through the common experiences of individuals like Marco, a representative of the misunderstood majority—the hourly workforce—that powers our economy. We've delved into the demographics, challenges, and misconceptions surrounding the hourly workforce, revealing a complex picture of resilience amid adversity. From the stark realities of financial insecurity to the nuances of the hiring process, it's clear that hourly workers navigate a landscape marked by significant hurdles. Yet, they remain the backbone of our daily lives and services.

It's clear the hourly workforce has significant depth and diversity. Far from the stereotypes of transient, inexperienced labor, this group encompasses a broad spectrum of ages, educational backgrounds, and aspirations, many of whom are juggling multiple jobs to support their families. The statistics are telling. With nearly 56 percent of the country's workforce being hourly, the sheer magnitude of this population underscores its importance. Yet, despite their numbers, hourly workers face systemic challenges—low wages, lack of emergency savings, and a high amount of debt—that speak to broader societal and economic issues.

The journey through the hiring process, as experienced by Marco, sheds light on the initial barriers many in the hourly workforce face. From the dehumanizing job hunt to the often impersonal and inefficient interview processes, it's evident there is a significant gap in how businesses approach and value potential hourly employees. This disconnect affects individual lives and reflects on the broader operational and ethical considerations businesses must address.

There are systemic issues at play, setting the stage for a broader discussion on the future of work and the imperative of addressing the hiring crisis in a post-COVID-19 world. The stories of hourly workers like Marco are not just anecdotes; they are a call to action for businesses, policymakers, and society at large to reevaluate and reform our approach to employment, equity, and economic security.

Next, we'll explore how the COVID-19 pandemic has undeniably intensified the hiring crisis, placing unprecedented strains on the hourly workforce. We'll discuss the evolving dynamics of the labor market, the heightened vulnerabilities faced by hourly workers, and the critical need for innovative solutions. In navigating the postpandemic landscape, understanding the depth of these challenges is crucial for building a more inclusive, equitable, and resilient workforce.

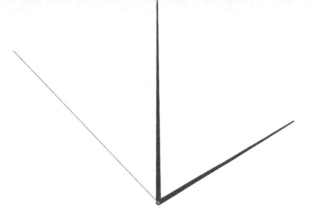

CHAPTER 2

The Hiring Crisis

So, how did we get to where we are today, with so many challenges facing hourly workers and those who employ them? There are several layers to the answer, two of which are crucial to look into further if we are to understand the root of the problem: an outdated process and an unprecedented pandemic.

A Process Stuck in the Past

Businesses have put their trust in the traditional hiring process for hundreds of years. It's the "tried and true" way to turn applicants into employees, with rigid guidelines and rules that must be adhered to. It just makes sense. Candidate tested, manager approved. Even if times changed, the hiring crisis was not the time to mess with the status quo.

So, businesses held firmly to their belief in the traditional hiring system and repeatedly emptied their pockets on sponsored job ads in an attempt to attract better candidates than before. In some cases, they were paying for the same applicants as before without realizing it. Instead of leveraging their current database and reviving interest from their "Applicant Graveyard" with plenty of untapped potential, they continued the cycle of paying expensive job board bills without any quality hires to show for it.

A lot of companies are still stuck in this mindset today due to the Applicant Flow Fallacy. They may see a high volume of applications populating their applicant tracking systems, but many of them are likely low-intent job seekers or duplicates.

It wasn't just money they were losing either. Now, managers have lost significantly more time due to a rapid increase in ghosting. People have started applying for opportunities faster than ever before, and managers are either too overwhelmed to review résumés or don't realize the importance of contacting top candidates as soon as possible. So, job seekers go with whichever company is lucky enough to reach them first, and the rest of the managers are forgotten or ignored.

In the same market where business owners complain about not being able to find quality workers, applicants cite their number one obstacle to finding work as "not getting interviews." I'm sure you've seen people from both sides voice their frustrations in the media and on social platforms. But who is actually at fault for this unprecedented problem? I challenge you to consider the idea that it might be neither the applicants nor the managers.

Let me paint the picture from both sides of the hiring equation.

Kaliyah needs to find a job. She's nineteen and goes to college full-time but struggles to cover the cost of textbooks. She wants to get ahead of the student loans looming over her head. Hoping to work evening shifts at one of the convenience stores in town, she does what all her friends do to find jobs. She takes out her phone, sets up an account on a job board site, and starts submitting applications to all the stores nearby with open positions.

A day goes by without any responses. Then a week, and another after that. Pretty soon, it's been a month without a word from any hiring managers. She logs back in to the job board and submits twice as many applications as before. It's becoming more dire for her to find extra work. Still nothing. Why is it so hard to get a job when many businesses need workers? Surely, they'd want the help she'd gladly provide, especially for night shifts that are typically less desirable. The job search continues as her frustration increases. Eventually, she hears from someone and accepts the offer without hesitation, forgetting about all the other companies she applied to.

Desmond needs to hire someone. He's fifty-two and has owned and operated a convenience store for twenty years now. An employee just quit on the spot, and he's been having to pick up the slack when others can't. Normally, this wouldn't be a problem. Desmond has dealt with situations like this numerous times, and it's typically no problem finding someone new to fill the position. However, the hiring crisis has made this a formidable task recently. It took him nearly two months to hire that person who didn't even last a week. The thought of going through all those tedious tasks in the hiring process again is daunting.

When he gets home one night after a double shift, Desmond decides to try advertising on a job board. The "Help Wanted" sign in the window of his store clearly isn't working. He creates an employer account, writes a job description, and boosts the promotion with their sponsored ads feature in the hopes that it will accelerate the process. A few days later, he logs back in and is relieved to see dozens of new applicants awaiting responses. His investment in sponsored ads seems to have paid off, that is, until he starts digging through the list.

The next day, he eagerly sifts through the résumés on his phone in between breaks and attending to customers. However, he quickly becomes overwhelmed with the sheer volume of applications to review while keeping up with his daily tasks at work. He's still understaffed and taking on extra responsibilities, after all.

Desmond wants to give everyone a fair shot, but exhaustion and impatience get the better of him. Kaliyah's résumé pops up on his screen, but some unconscious bias kicks in when he sees her non-white-sounding name and moves on to the next applicant without even thinking. Finally, he goes with his gut and chooses a few applicants he believes look good on paper. He reaches out in the morning, but none of them respond. Then he tries contacting a handful more. Still nothing. Don't they want to work here? Why would they apply if it wasn't the case?

He goes back and checks the bill for how much he paid to get all those applicants who just ghosted him. It's a shock to his mind and his credit card, but he pays the bill and sets up even more sponsored job ads, continuing the cycle. He needs the help, after all. Maybe the next batch of applicants will be better.

So, we have two opposing stories from either side. Kaliyah can't believe how hard it is to get a manager to contact her, let alone get an interview when businesses should be desperate to hire someone like her. Desmond can't believe how hard it is to review such a high volume of applications properly and get in touch with someone who seems like a good fit, even though he's desperate for the help that someone like Kaliyah would provide. Again, who is at fault?

Let's dive into the hourly hiring scene pre- and post-COVID-19 to see if the root of the problem is actually in the traditional hiring process we've used for years and continue to use, despite proof that it's ineffective and, for lack of a better word, broken.

How COVID-19 Forever Changed the Landscape

It's pretty hard, borderline impossible, to deny that the COVID-19 pandemic had a significant impact on how businesses hire and retain hourly employees. I've personally had more conversations than I can count with owners who mention the pandemic when discussing their hiring challenges. I'm sure I'll continue to have conversations like these, and I'll continue to empathize with their situations while guiding them toward new solutions that solve these unprecedented challenges.

I'm also certain there's no going back to how things were in the hourly workforce before the pandemic. But when you think about it, was it really that much better? While the situation has certainly gotten worse and transformed in ways nobody could've predicted, let's be honest: it wasn't all sunshine and rainbows beforehand.

The process for hiring hourly employees was already fundamentally flawed, and the pandemic exposed the cracks in a strained system that was on the verge of crumbling anyway.

Let's think back to when people flipped through newspapers or had to go into their local restaurants or grocery stores to find work. They may have seen a "Now Hiring" sign in the window or just decided to try their luck, grabbing an application from whoever would pay them attention inside. They would deal with first-impression bias right off the bat and then sit down to fill out a sheet of paper that would end up buried in the back office, never to be seen again. They'd repeat this process at as many locations as possible before returning home to wait for a ring from the phone or a ding from their email inbox.

Keep in mind this was just for those who had reliable transportation, access to a computer, and the free time to complete several applications and make it to interviews. Many people, especially members of the hourly workforce, lack at least one of these requirements for securing work, limiting job seekers' opportunities and stifling applicant flow for businesses.

Fast-forward to the peak of the pandemic. When COVID-19 was at its worst, so was unemployment. In what has been nicknamed the "Great Resignation," unemployment skyrocketed from 3.5 to 14.7 percent[4] as employees left jobs due to health concerns or layoffs.

Suddenly, the "invisible workforce" became the highlight of news stories and headlines, with more leverage than ever before. Businesses were in a state of shock and disarray as they tried to figure out how to actively attract the applicants they once had a surplus of without much investment in recruitment efforts.

Many companies took a page out of the sports playbook to recruit workers quickly. They offered sign-on bonuses for new employees, which was particularly popular among job seekers. Amazon advertised $1,000 sign-on bonuses[5] for employees in some states, with an additional $100 if they showed proof of a COVID-19 vaccination.

---

4   US Bureau of Labor Statistics, "Civilian Unemployment Rate—Seasonally Adjusted," accessed February 6, 2024, https://www.bls.gov/charts/employment-situation/civilian-unemployment-rate.htm.

5   Business Insider, "Amazon Is Hiring 75,000 Workers with $1,000 Signing Bonuses. Here's How to Apply," accessed February 6, 2024, https://www.businessinsider.com/amazon-hiring-75000-workers-1000-signing-bonuses-how-to-apply-2021-5.

Certain McDonald's franchisees paid new employees $500[6] and were willing to give $50 to anyone who would simply attend an interview. Companies introduced several other new benefits for hourly workers during this time, including daily pay, college tuition reimbursement, career pathways, and better health insurance.

If that isn't proof of the desperation these businesses were feeling, I don't know what is. It's also evidence of a much greater shift that shook society during the height of the pandemic. Hourly workers suddenly had leverage over potential employers, which was a complete reversal of the dynamic we'd seen historically before the hiring crisis. Job seekers had the freedom to choose from more opportunities than ever before, and they gained the ability to negotiate terms of employment. Business owners were now the ones feeling the pressure to hire people quickly and stay afloat, while others limited their hours or shut down completely.

Then, almost as quickly as it increased, the unemployment rate plummeted from 14.7 percent back down to 3.5 percent[7] when job seekers flooded back into the market. That's a greater fluctuation than occurred in the Great Depression, and it happened twice within the span of two years. As if these radical shifts weren't enough to destabilize the labor market, the number of job openings also surpassed the number of unemployed workers.[8]

---

6   Business Insider, "Fast Food Chains Like McDonald's, Taco Bell, and Subway Are Hiring as the Industry Grapples with a Labor Shortage," accessed February 6, 2024, https://www.businessinsider.com/ fast-food-chains-hiring-mcdonalds-taco-bell-subway-jobs-2021-5.

7   US Bureau of Labor Statistics, "Civilian Unemployment Rate—Seasonally Adjusted."

8   US Bureau of Labor Statistics, "More Job Openings Than Unemployed People since May 2021," accessed February 6, 2024, https://www.bls.gov/opub/ ted/2023/more-job-openings-than-unemployed-people-since-may-2021.htm.

So even if everyone who was unemployed got a job, the workforce still couldn't keep up with demand. It felt like progress, but problems persisted. Something had to change.

How COVID-Specific "Solutions" Created New Long-Lasting Problems

Business owners were desperate for a solution that could help them achieve optimal staffing levels, which put pressure on HR tech providers and job boards to support their clients. They introduced reactionary features like "one-click apply" to boost applicant flow by removing friction from the application process. This seemed to be the answer everyone was looking for … until it wasn't.

Almost overnight, people went from applying to a *few* jobs per day to submitting *dozens* of applications in minutes. It sounded like a win-win for understaffed businesses and job seekers, but this wasn't the case. While job seekers were relieved they no longer had to spend hours on lengthy applications, and hiring managers were grateful to see the surge of interest in open positions, the honeymoon phase of this "solution" was short-lived.

It wasn't long before people realized these quick-apply features created more problems than they solved. The sudden influx of applications was a burden masked as a benefit. Applicant flow quickly went from a *volume* problem to a *conversion* problem as managers struggled to keep up. Business owners thought they needed more applicants even though they really just needed to get better at converting the ones they already had into employees.

I recently conducted a study with my company, Sprockets, that included data from more than 540,000 applicants in the hourly workforce across 305 business locations, which uncovered some shocking findings that support this idea.[9] A particularly noteworthy one is that only 18 percent of applications ever get viewed by managers. And from there, only 3 percent of applicants actually become employees.

We also found that it takes an average of 8.8 days for managers to contact applicants. Why would they ignore so many candidates and then take so long to contact them when they so desperately need to hire workers? Paradoxically, it might be the fact that they are understaffed that creates a vicious cycle of not being able to hire new employees. They are overworked and exhausted, and they lack the tools to review so many applications effectively.

The Impact of Today's Generational Gaps

Now, if I told my dad I would apply to several jobs and then not show up to interviews when I was a teenager, he'd never let me live it down. But times have changed, and while it can certainly be frustrating, employers shouldn't take it personally when a candidate ghosts them. A helpful exercise is to put yourself in the mind of a seventeen-year-old.

You're eager to land your first job but get overwhelmed by the number of opportunities, nervous at the thought of an interview, and need to coordinate travel. For a teenager to go through this process for every single place they apply to is a tough ask. The same goes for applicants who expect more from managers. They must understand how overworked and overwhelmed they are and not take it personally when they don't get an immediate response.

---

9   Sprockets, "Case Study: Applicant Drop-Off," accessed February 6, 2024, https://sprockets.ai/case-study-applicant-drop-off/.

Let's go back to the stories of Kaliyah, the frustrated job seeker who can't seem to get an interview, and Desmond, the overwhelmed business owner who can't seem to get in touch with any quality candidates.

One is a college student in her late teens, and the other is an experienced business owner in his fifties. This might not have been significant to point out in the years before COVID-19 and the resulting hiring crisis, but generational gaps have become a much bigger deal. We can see it in how they approach the hiring process. Kaliyah goes straight to her smartphone and takes advantage of the click-to-apply feature to maximize her chances of landing a job, while Desmond initially relies on a "Help Wanted" sign before resorting to sponsored ads online.

Kaliyah constantly checks her phone, hoping she'll get a notification from her app any minute. Desmond focuses on his work responsibilities and only checks his account when he gets home at the end of the night if he has the time and isn't too exhausted. Unfortunately, this means he doesn't review résumés or reach out to his applicants as quickly as they'd like, and many of them lose interest or accept other opportunities by the time he tries to contact them.

Another study my team and I conducted about applicants' expectations found that speed is of the utmost importance in the hiring process.[10] The hourly workforce is largely made up of millennials and Gen Zers, like Kaliyah, who want to hear from managers quickly and stay hyperconnected. According to the 566 applicants we surveyed, the three most important aspects of the hiring process included a fast response after an interview, a fast reply to their application, and a quick, easy application process.

10   Sprockets, "Case Study: Applicant Expectations," accessed February 6, 2024, https://sprockets.ai/case-study-applicant-expectations/.

We also found that 50 percent of hourly workers said they expect to hear from potential employers within three days, and 11 percent want to be contacted within twenty-four hours. That puts a lot of pressure on owners and managers like Desmond, who take an average of 8.8 days to contact applicants. There must be some way for us to bridge the generational gaps that keep widening and bringing the labor market to another crisis point.

Why There's a Lack of Solutions Today

As someone who has unprecedented access to product leaders in this space, whether HR technology providers or investment vehicles, I've continually pondered why these problems persist despite vast technological advancements. Artificial intelligence, big data, and automation have progressed in other industries with leaps and bounds, yet in human resources departments that drive much of our people practices, technology has been largely untouched. Why is that? How can we put a man on the moon and double the average life expectancy[11] but have the worst employee turnover and discrimination in hiring than ever before?

It's because of another gap that I've personally experienced and struggled to overcome for years. In addition to the mismatch in mindsets between generations in today's workforce, there seems to be a significant gap between creating a solution and commercializing it in the hiring space, especially when that solution is tech-based.

When I built the hiring software to help businesses solve their issues with recruiting and retaining high-quality employees, my efforts were met with a surprising amount of opposition. After several failed attempts at pitching the software that I knew would positively impact

---

11   Our World in Data, "Life Expectancy," accessed February 6, 2024, https://ourworldindata.org/life-expectancy#life-expectancy-has-improved-globally.

these businesses, I came to an eye-opening yet very disappointing realization. There are two facets of innovation: building and adoption. And you must have these two vital pieces of the puzzle to achieve progress.

In other words, you need to have a good product and a market that is willing to invest in it. This market is a tough one to crack. Even if they understood they had hiring challenges, business leaders were more willing to deal with them than accept the idea of a tech-based solution.

This friction is charged with a capitalistic complication: In general, HR tech is historically uninvestable. While the asset classes of angel, venture, and private equity firms have different measurements of success, all groups want their portfolios to do one thing: grow. And they want the growth to be quick. Investors don't see how investing in tech services that benefit the hourly workforce can make that happen. Even though business leaders and investment firms will agree there's a problem, the nature of the market simply makes solutions not seem worthwhile.

This phenomenon is understood and lived out intimately in venture capital. Every year, advantageous funds, institutions, and individuals invest billions of dollars in technology companies. It's highly competitive. In fact, only 0.05 percent of start-ups get venture capital funding.[12] The criterion for these financing rounds is a combination of "unit economics" that showcase the scalability of future growth and the eventual enterprise value multipliers that determine company worth over time.

Depending on the fund thesis, these unit economic requirements vary. However, there are common metrics that a business must have to join the elite, namely growth, gross margin, and user retention. When they are all strong, the combination of these three things shows potential investors that your business can grow customers, keep them,

---

12   Fundera, "Startup Funding Statistics," accessed February 6, 2024, https://www.fundera.com/resources/startup-funding-statistics.

and, most importantly, make money from their subscriptions. Technology companies that do these things well get funded, innovate, and grow quickly in their respective markets. Technology companies that don't are left on the bench, largely underfunded and under-resourced to scale.

Admittedly, when I first started an HR technology company and approached the venture capital community with the crazy idea to service the hourly workforce, I felt like the kid from the movie *Final Destination*. It opens with a man who experiences a vision of the plane crashing, and he frantically tries to get his friends and other passengers off the plane before takeoff. He screams and pleads until, finally, a flight attendant rips him from his seat and sends him back to the terminal. Minutes later, the plane blows up.

I have a similar experience in learning and sharing information about the invisible workforce. I saw the harrowing statistics, studied the market opportunity intimately, and had enough early proof points that the product worked and that we could be the market leader very quickly. I remember pounding my fist on table after table in San Francisco, trying to convince investors that I saw something others did not. At the time, I couldn't understand why every investment in every firm wasn't addressing this problem. It's the problem of a lifetime to solve. It is of massive scale. It will make a significant impact on real people.

So, you can imagine my surprise when I picked up the official narrative of the investment community: "We hear you, but this space is uninvestable."

What? Why?

The same response across literally 104 meetings: "To do this right, you need the small and medium-sized business (SMB) space, which has way too much churn and too hard of a sales cycle."

They were right. Selling software to SMBs can present various challenges, and these challenges can arise from several factors:

- *Limited Budgets:* SMBs often operate with tighter budgets compared to larger enterprises. They may prioritize spending on immediate needs, making it challenging to invest in software solutions, especially if the perceived return on investment is unclear.

- *Limited Resources:* SMBs typically have smaller teams and fewer resources. Implementing new software may require time and effort that they can't easily spare, particularly if the software requires training or customization.

- *Lack of IT Expertise:* Many SMBs may not have dedicated IT staff or sophisticated IT infrastructure. They might be less comfortable adopting new technologies, especially if they lack the expertise to integrate and maintain the software.

- *Resistance to Change:* SMBs may be more resistant to change, especially if they have established processes that seem to be working for them. Introducing new software often involves disrupting existing workflows, and some businesses may be hesitant to embrace that change.

- *Complex Decision-Making Processes:* In SMBs, decision-making processes are often more centralized, and key decision-makers may wear multiple hats within the organization. This can lead to longer sales cycles as you navigate through the decision-making hierarchy.

- *Customization and Integration Concerns:* SMBs may worry about the complexity and cost of customizing or integrating new software with their existing systems. They may prefer solutions that are easy to implement without extensive IT support.

- *Perceived Risk:* Smaller businesses may perceive adopting new software as risky. They may fear disruptions to their operations, data security issues, or the potential for the software not meeting their specific needs.

- *Limited Brand Recognition:* If you are a smaller or newer software vendor without widespread brand recognition, gaining trust and credibility can be challenging. SMBs may be more inclined to choose well-established brands with a track record.

- *Education and Awareness:* Some SMBs may not be aware of the potential benefits of certain software solutions or may lack understanding of how these tools could address their specific pain points. Effective education and communication are crucial in overcoming this hurdle.

The challenge with SMBs goes beyond selling.

Servicing SMBs, from a customer service perspective, is especially difficult. They are notoriously harsh on software companies and, despite their size, oftentimes expect white-glove service. When something glitches or there's a natural hiccup, SMBs are quick to "churn" and even quicker to stop payments.

There's a meme that floats around the technology founder community about accounts receivable. It shows two emails.

1. SMB customer that received an invoice for $99. "Hello [company], I just received your invoice. Are you able to send me a detailed ROI for this subscription? I'd like to know what you did, the account activity, and when our contract is up immediately."

2. Enterprise customer that received an invoice for $99,000. "Received. Paid. Thanks."

SMBs have very high expectations for the execution and fast delivery of their software providers, which is completely fair. However, it does not create a strong environment for an emerging, venture-backed technology start-up that needs to sell and retain customers at scale. As a result, many of the fastest-growing and most powerful technologies stay away from this category altogether.

Joint Employer

Big brand operators in the franchise model make up a large portion of the would-be target audience for these types of innovations since they employ millions of hourly workers in industries like fast-food and home services with high employee turnover.

Franchising was one of the earliest business models that made the American dream seem attainable. The asset class famously struggled at managing the franchisor/franchisee model when it exclusively recruited established, affluent businesspeople at the very beginning. At the time, these individuals opted to play by their own rules, serve their own menus, and develop their own operational playbooks. The pioneers knew that for the franchise model to scale, standardization couldn't be a "nice to have." It needed to be a requirement.

Although likely exaggerated a bit in the movie "The Founder," there's truth in that some big brands shifted their attention to more middle-class operators that would scrape together just enough money to build a location and follow corporate's directions to a T. The operators that flourished and scaled from one to ten to hundreds of locations were those that followed these principles and developed intense rigor around the standardization of processes, menus, uniforms, you name it.

In 2015, I spoke with the CEO of a major hotel brand who told me, "When you're in one of my rooms, and you draw the blinds, I want you to have no idea where you are in the world." He and his brand partners wanted each room to look, smell, and feel the same. It didn't matter if that particular location was owned by corporate or a franchisee. His expectation was high-quality service that was uniform. No exceptions.

As consumers, we expect that. We crave it. How would you feel if you got off a highway during a long drive to eat at your favorite Chinese restaurant only to find out that the operator didn't make their signature orange chicken? Could you imagine walking into a gym that didn't have treadmills? The American population has grown accustomed to the products, services, and amenities that continuously lead to year-over-year growth in the franchise vertical.

Franchising in no way guarantees success as a franchise owner/ operator. However, it provides a remarkable structure for success, even for those with only a basic level of business experience. As a result, it attracts a specific type of entrepreneur who expects a certain level of guidance and support. These operators often have the entrepreneurial resources and gusto to make an independent business work on its own, but they have elected to enter a system where they are told what to serve, where to buy wholesale goods, and how to advertise them. If they didn't, these franchisees could, in theory, elect to open their own restaurant, hotel, or homecare facilities. Starting "AJ's Burger Joint" would be very different from a well-established quick-service restaurant.

Despite the franchise category's successful model of standardization, franchisors hesitate to inform or mandate one thing. Can you guess what that is? It's not the menu, equipment, TV ads, or uniforms. Guidelines on those are given in the franchisee handbook.

Wait for it… it's people practices. This is in large part due to legislation.

In 2020, the federal government released legislation called "Joint Employer." The term "Joint Employer" refers to a situation in which two or more employers share control and responsibility over the same employee or group of employees. This concept is particularly relevant in employment and labor law, and it can have implications for issues such as liability for wage and hour violations, employment discrimination, and other workplace-related matters.

Depending on your political position, your impression of Joint Employer may vary. However, there's little debate as to the scale of its impact.

Legal talk aside, franchisors have explained it to me bluntly: If an employee sues their employer in a franchisee's business, the corporate entity could be held responsible for the franchisee's people practices if they, the corporate entity, mandated them. Corporate entities don't want to be held liable because one of their franchisees hired illegally or terminated someone wrongfully, litigation that happens regularly in this hourly workforce.

Do you see a fundamental problem yet?

There are an estimated 8.7 million workers employed by business operators in the franchise model that are hardwired to operate with a handbook.[13] However, the Joint Employer law makes franchisors shy away from providing the hypothetical chapter on "people." This leaves arguably the most complicated, legally charged, and difficult part of the business at the mercy of the franchise operator. Franchisors don't always feel comfortable giving franchisees guidance on how to conduct their hiring or people processes, even if it would drastically improve their recruitment and retention rates. The fear of backlash outweighs the promise of success due to innovation.

I understand this pain intimately, as I've been selling hiring and human resource software to franchises for close to a decade. There's

13   PR Newswire, "2023 Economic Outlook Shows Franchise Job and Unit Growth Trends Ahead of Pre-Pandemic Levels," accessed February 6, 2024, https://www.prnewswire.com/news-releases/2023-economic-outlook-shows-franchise-job-and-unit-growth-trends-ahead-of-pre-pandemic-levels-301782808.html.

amazing work being done by world-class and passionate executives in corporate franchising. However, Joint Employer is seen to many as a restricting force in scaling best practices to those operators that may need them most.

However, the lack of formal structure here is neither inherently good nor bad. Numerous franchisees use the flexibility to develop amazing programs.

In fact, some franchise operators join the asset class because all they want to do is service the hourly workers. These groups invest heavily in their people, far beyond any corporate requirements or expectations. In Kendall, Florida, a Chick-fil-A operator offers FTEs a three-day workweek to encourage a work-life balance unprecedented in this workforce.[14] In Springfield, Missouri, a Wendy's operator rewards their team members for good grades and even developed an onsite home program where employees can spend time on the job completing their school assignments.[15]

However, there are also franchise operators who do not prioritize their workers and struggle without corporate mandates. The US Department of Labor regularly fines franchisees at the biggest brands for child labor, discrimination, and other workforce-related challenges.

Every policy and law comes with pros and cons. It's important for all franchise businesses to understand the Joint Employer laws,

---

14   Bill Murphy Jr., "Chick-fil-A Just Introduced a 3-Day Work Week. People Think It's the 'Best Idea Ever,'" *Inc.*, January 31, 2023, https://www.inc.com/bill-murphy-jr/chick-fil-a-just-introduced-a-3-day-work-week-people-think-its-best-idea-ever.html.

15   Danny Klein, "Why One Franchise Group Is Paying Employees to Do Homework in Restaurants," *QSR* magazine, January 31, 2023, https://www.qsrmagazine.com/story/why-one-franchise-group-is-paying-employees-to-do-homework-in-restaurants/.

and I always recommend speaking with an attorney if this impacts your business.

Key Takeaways

At this point, we have navigated the intricate realities facing job seekers and employers in today's labor market. There is a clear disconnect between the supply and demand of the workforce, exemplified by the stories of Kaliyah and Desmond, each struggling on opposite ends of the hiring process. This narrative underscores a crucial paradox: While businesses urgently seek quality hires, potential employees face significant barriers to even securing an interview. In addition, the pandemic's role as both a disruptor and an accelerator of existing trends has laid bare the inadequacies of the old ways, propelling the hourly workforce into the spotlight and demanding urgent, innovative solutions.

We've seen how the rapid adoption of technology, while seemingly a boon for both employers and job seekers, has introduced its own set of challenges. Features like "one-click-apply" have transformed applicant flow from a quantity issue to a quality and conversion crisis, with a staggering majority of applications never even viewed by hiring managers. This, coupled with the generational gaps in expectations and the rapid pace of the hiring process, has further complicated the landscape, leaving businesses and job seekers alike in a state of frustration and disconnect.

Moreover, this chapter illuminates the lack of investment and adoption of technological solutions in the HR space, a critical gap that hinders the progress toward more efficient, equitable hiring practices. Despite the clear need for innovation, systemic barriers, such as the challenges of selling and servicing SMBs and the intricacies of the franchise model, sometimes stymie the implementation of potentially transformative solutions.

Businesses should not only care about the issues facing hourly workers but also recognize the profound impact these challenges have on their bottom lines. The narratives of Kaliyah and Desmond, the broader systemic issues, and the failure to adopt new solutions not only affect individual lives but also directly influence the operational success, brand reputation, and financial health of businesses.

The next chapter will delve into the tangible benefits of addressing the hiring crisis, from improving employee retention to enhancing productivity and customer satisfaction. Investing in innovative hiring solutions and prioritizing the well-being of the hourly workforce are not just ethical imperatives but strategic business decisions that can lead to sustainable success in an increasingly competitive and fast-paced market.

CHAPTER 3

Why Businesses Should Care

Treating hourly workers poorly isn't just bad for humanity; it's horrendous for your business performance. With turnover in the hourly workforce exceeding 100 percent annually, this is an unfortunate and expensive common occurrence. These costs and measures are oftentimes underreported and misunderstood; however, in this chapter we explore the true impact of how it's killing your business.

Long before the sun rises, George wakes up to the sharp sound of his alarm clock so he can punch the clock at work for another strenuous shift at a fast-food restaurant. It's been weeks since he's had a day off, but he needs the money, especially now that he has hospital bills he can't afford. He gets up, puts on his uniform, eyes the pile of overdue bills on the counter, and pours a quick cup of coffee before rushing over to the bus stop to get to work on time so he doesn't get docked an hour of pay again for being a few minutes late.

He wears a fake smile and walks through the door to start another day just like every other. He mops the floor, wipes down the tables, scrubs the toilets, and cleans himself up before taking his spot at the cash register. Oh, how he hates the ding that door makes every single time a customer enters and the squeak it makes as it closes behind them. Fake smile. Warm greeting. Enter order. Thank you. Repeat.

George just hopes he can make it through the day with fewer customers complaining to him than the day before. Don't they know he's just one person trying to do the work of several crew members? Today is even worse since someone called out of work who was supposed to help him on the register. His fake smile weakens as he rings up more customers and listens to more complaints.

Whenever he gets a few minutes between customers, the manager gives him constant reminders to stay busy. Clean this. Fix that. Smile more. George thinks back to when he applied for this job. The description read, "Exciting opportunity with great benefits and a positive culture!" He sighs. None of those promises were true. This job is the opposite of exciting, the benefits are less than what most people can live on, and the culture definitely isn't positive.

George thinks more about it during his one and only fifteen-minute break toward the end of the night by the dumpsters out back. He doesn't mind, though, because it's the only place he can be alone for a bit and get some "fresh" air without having to deal with customers or listen to the constant gossip from coworkers in the kitchen. Taking out his cell phone, he scrolls through a job site and sees there's an opening at another restaurant nearby that pays one more dollar per hour. Apply. He hears a shout from inside—his manager telling him to get back on the register (with some colorful language). So, he ashes his cigarette and walks inside that restaurant for the last time.

"I quit."

Let's take a step back for a second. Why should businesses care when this happens? They made the conscious decision to enter a high-turnover industry, and hourly positions aren't viewed as pathways to long-term careers, so there's no expectation for workers to stay. Managers can fill their role with the next applicant in line.

That's one way to think about the situation, but is it the correct one? Excuse the cliché, but what most people see here is just the tip of the iceberg. The consequences of overlooking hourly workers like George go much deeper than you might initially think.

How Turnover Compounds

The obvious consequence is how miserable George was due to poor work conditions and that he struggled to make ends meet with what was not a livable wage. It goes much further, though. For instance, what about the employees left behind at the restaurant to pick up the slack? It's not George's fault he was tired of being mistreated and opted for a job that paid more so he could catch up on his hospital bills (or any expenses, for that matter). Until his position is filled, which can take several days or weeks, everyone else needs to pitch in. They'll be taking on additional tasks and working double shifts, leading to burnout and possible resignation.

Moving up the chain, we now have a manager who must scramble to find a suitable replacement using a hiring process that's time-consuming and ineffective. It can take countless hours of reviewing résumés and conducting interviews, many of whom end up wasting their time or ghosting them entirely when they could've been focusing on important daily operations. Plus, all those customer complaints that George had to deal with? Double them. Along with the bad reviews that hurt the restaurant's reputation and potential repeat business.

Cost of Turnover

Turnover also costs businesses a shocking amount of money. It can cost anywhere from $1,500 to $10,000 to replace a single hourly employee when you take into account the lost productivity, recruitment costs, and training time.[16] Now, consider how often this happens at C-stores or restaurants with annual turnover rates of 130–150 percent. That cost adds up quickly, especially for people who own several locations. So, you have franchisees and business owners paying an unbelievable amount of money every year for turnover that, for the most part, is preventable. Year after year, they use the same broken hiring process and accept the cost to their bottom lines, essentially hindering their potential growth. It adds up to an estimated $1 trillion annual cost in voluntary turnover for businesses in the United States.[17]

Employee turnover also occurs more rapidly than some might think, meaning those costs add up very quickly. One study found that 33 percent of employees leave within ninety days of starting a job, meaning one in three people hired today will be gone in three

---

16   Midlands Technical College, "Measuring the Real Cost of Employee Turnover," accessed February 7, 2024, https://www.midlandstech.edu/news/measuring-real-cost-employee-turnover.

17   Ibid.

months.[18] However, your turnover rate could be even higher than that. The initial ninety-day period has been called "the magic window"[19] that shows employers whether or not an employee will be a good fit.[20]

Marissa Andrada, chief people officer of Chipotle, recently told the *Wall Street Journal*, "If you see someone hit the three-month mark, the reality is, they're going to be here for at least a year." Three months gives employers plenty of time to evaluate workers, almost like an extended interview, and workers have a chance to get into a routine and decide if they'd like to stay long term. (Workers often figure this out within the first couple of weeks.)

Ultimately, if you could improve your hiring process and increase ninety-day employee retention, you're boosting annual retention and drastically reducing turnover costs. That can add up to a lot of savings, especially in industries like fast-food service, which averages over 130 percent annual turnover.

18   G&A Partners, "Why an Employee's First 90 Days Are Make or Break," accessed February 7, 2024, https://www.gnapartners.com/resources/articles/why-an-employees-first-90-days-are-make-or-break.

19   *The Wall Street Journal*, "Bosses Swear by the 90-Day Rule to Keep Workers Long-Term," accessed February 7, 2024, https://www.wsj.com/articles/bosses-swear-by-the-90-day-rule-to-keep-workers-long-term-11656153431.

20   Dharmesh Shah, "Why 33% of New Employees Quit in 90 Days," *Psychology Today*, March 12, 2019, https://www.psychologytoday.com/us/blog/platform-success/201903/why-33-percent-new-employees-quit-in-90-days.

Calculating the Impact of Turnover at Your Business

So, how do you calculate this important metric?
Here's a step-by-step guide to find out:

1. Record the number of employees you have at the beginning of the period.
2. Record the number of employees you have ninety days later.
3. Add these numbers, then divide by 2. This is your average employee count.

$$\left(\begin{array}{l} \text{Employee Count at Beginning of Time Period} \\ \text{+ Employee Count at the End of Time Period} \end{array} \right) \div 2 = \textbf{Average Employee Count}$$

4. Then, record the number of employees who left (both voluntarily and involuntarily) at the end of the ninety-day period.
5. Divide this number by your average employee count, and then multiply the quotient by 100. This is your ninety-day employee turnover rate as a percentage.

$$\left(\begin{array}{l} \text{Employees Who Left in Time Period} \\ \text{+ Average Employee Count} \end{array} \right) \times 100 = \textbf{Employee Turnover \%}$$

The estimated cost of turnover varies depending on the job, industry, and where you get your data. For example, NACS says it costs \$1,341 to replace a full-time convenience store associate.[21] According to PeopleKeep, it can cost \$1,500 to replace hourly

---

21 "Here's How to Intelligently Reduce Employee Turnover," Convenience Store News, March 17, 2022, https://www.convenience.org/Media/Daily/2022/Mar/17/2-Heres-Intelligent-Reduce-Employee-Turnover_Tech.

workers.[22] An article by SHRM says it's $4,969.[23] The Center for Hospitality Research at Cornell puts it at $5,864 for the frontline hotel employees when accounting for costs associated with predeparture, recruiting, selection, training, and productivity loss.[24]

What does this mean to an actual business's bottom line? Let's say you run a restaurant group with ten locations and fifty employees at each one. With an average replacement cost of $1,500 and a turnover rate of 144 percent, you'd be losing $1,080,000 annually. If you run a single call center with 250 employees and we use the estimate of $4,969 with 150 percent turnover, you'd lose $2,484,500 each year on employee turnover alone. Let that sink in.

Industry	# of Employees Per Location	Business Locations	Find and Replace Cost	Turnover Rate	Cost of Turnover
Restaurant	50	10	$1,500	144%	$1,080,000
Hotel	25	5	$5,864	130%	$952,900
Convenience Store	5	75	$1,341	150%	$754,313
Call Center	250	1	$4,969	200%	$2,484,500
Care Facility	40	6	$4,969	180%	$2,146,608

22   PeopleKeep, "Employee Retention: The Real Cost of Losing an Employee," PeopleKeep, accessed February 19, 2024, https://www.peoplekeep.com/blog/employee-retention-the-real-cost-of-losing-an-employee.

23   Roy Maurer, "Employers Struggle to Hire Hourly Workers; Turnover Rises," SHRM, January 10, 2023, https://www.shrm.org/topics-tools/news/talent-acquisition/employers-struggle-to-hire-hourly-workers-turnover-rises.

24   Michael Luca and Georgios Zervas, "Fake It till You Make It: Reputation, Competition, and Yelp Review Fraud," Harvard Business School NOM Unit Working Paper No. 14-006, 2016, https://papers.ssrn.com/sol3/papers.cfm?abstract_id=2293164.

Cost of "Quiet Quitting"

Now, what happens when someone is unhappy but they *don't* quit? It's expensive to replace employees who actually quit, but what has been called "quiet quitting" can have a negative impact on your bottom line too.[25] This is when employees are not engaged and just do the bare minimum. Companies that treat their employees well will see a positive return on investment in the realms of engagement, productivity, retention, and their bottom lines. Those who don't invest in the health and well-being of their employees will get negative results, which may, unfortunately, seem like the norm at some workplaces today, making them essentially unnoticeable to employers. Customers and team members will definitely notice, though.

Haven't you ever been in a situation where you've interacted with frontline employees who clearly hate their jobs? What about the times you've had pleasant interactions with bubbly employees who enjoy their work? We've all been there, whether we're the ones who hate our jobs, love our jobs, or are the customers interacting with them. It happens. Although, one should happen more often than the other if you catch my drift.

We have so many interactions with frontline workers on a daily basis—more than most of us even realize. What if all those interactions were positive? Think about the impact that it would have on your day-to-day life. Think about the impact it would have on *their* daily lives, the misunderstood majority. Now, think about how negative workplaces impact everyone. That might be closer to the reality we live in today, unfortunately. The difference could come

25   Jim Harter, "Is 'Quiet Quitting' for Real?," Gallup, September 1, 2022, https://www.gallup.com/workplace/398306/quiet-quitting-real.aspx.

down to whether employers make a conscious effort to create an environment that fosters positivity or not.

Here's a hypothetical scenario to help illustrate this point. You're the owner of a hotel, and while I'm not sure which you'd choose when asked if you'd like the good news or bad news first, let's suppose you opt for the second option. The bad news is that your manager hired an employee, and they're not so happy with the workplace. Maybe they had a poor experience throughout the hiring process, perhaps the job isn't what they expected based on the job description, or they might not have been set up for success in the training process.

It could even be the case that they aren't the right fit for your hotel. Whatever the reason, they aren't happy. They lack motivation and show up to work each day a few minutes late in a wrinkly uniform and do the bare minimum when it comes to their tasks. Unfortunately, they are one of the first faces guests see when they visit your hotel, and it doesn't set the best first impression for their stay. No "Hello! How are you doing? What can I help you with?" All guests get when they approach the front desk is a disgruntled "Yeah?" That's not a great start for the customer experience.

When people from out of town ask for recommendations on where to eat nearby, all they get is, "There's a pizza place up the road." It's too bad because your hotel has an attached bar and restaurant, so you lose out on opportunities for additional revenue. When guests call down to the front desk to see if they can get more towels or amenities, it often takes hours to reach them. That pretty much seals the deal. You've lost out on potential revenue, missed any chance to get repeat customers, and received a scathing negative review online. Plus, word gets around, and they've told all their friends and family members to avoid staying at your hotel.

Could this situation have been avoided? Probably. Think about the difference it makes when your manager makes the right hiring decision, the new employee gets proper training, and they thrive in the positive work environment that you and your team have established. Your new customer service representative comes in each morning with a big smile on their face, ready to put that same smile on the faces of every guest they see walk through the door. They give each person a cheerful greeting, ask if they can answer any questions for them, and mention the delicious specials they can enjoy at your restaurant while handing them the room key.

"Don't hesitate to call me at the front desk if there's anything you need that could make your visit better. Thanks for staying with us!" All of the guests, dozens of them throughout the day, take this positivity with them as they relax in the room, indulge at your bar and restaurant, and tell friends how much they love your hotel. You've earned yourself extra revenue, repeat customers, and several positive reviews online. The employee goes home happy each day, as do the guests. And, of course, you can't complain as the hotel owner with the boost to your bottom line and reputation.

You don't need to move mountains to make this a reality. As I'll likely say throughout this book ad nauseam, seemingly small steps can make a big difference. And it's truly a win-win for everyone.

Cost of Bias

But hold on. I haven't even mentioned one of the biggest problems that is worsened by strain on managers. It's been rapidly gaining attention from the public and news outlets in recent years, although it should've been in the headlines long ago so businesses would've felt the pressure to address it sooner. I'm talking about bias in the hiring process. It can cost hundreds of thousands of dollars in lawsuits and actually limit your growth since more diverse teams are proven to be more effective and productive.

Bias has plagued the hiring process since, well, the first time someone ever applied for a job. As humans, we all have some level of inherent bias, whether conscious or unconscious. And as much as we'd all like to think we can truly give everyone a fair shot, it's not always that simple. In a recent study, 48 percent of HR managers admitted that bias affects which candidates they hire.[26] The hiring process as it stands today leaves far too much room for bias to creep in at each stage. The list goes on, but the point is that when humans are under-staffed, overwhelmed, and tired, it makes it easy for our unconscious biases to take over to some extent.

For example, managers may feel rushed to review résumés after working a long shift, opening the opportunity for unconscious bias to influence their decisions. A study from the Swiss research university ETH Zurich in 2021 found that recruiters' hiring bias increased by 20 percent just before lunch and near the end of the workday.[27] This research suggests factors like exhaustion may be linked to an increase in unconscious bias.

It can be introduced early on in the hiring process, specifically during the recruitment stage, if job descriptions or titles include gender-coded language.[28] This goes beyond the obvious usage of specific

---

26 Zippia, "Hiring Bias Statistics," accessed February 7, 2024, https://www.zippia.com/employer/hiring-bias-statistics/.

27 TechTarget, "Study Finds Hiring Bias by Recruiters, Especially Tired Ones," accessed February 7, 2024, https://www.techtarget.com/searchhrsoftware/news/252495310/Study-finds-hiring-bias-by-recruiters-especially-tired-ones.

28 Harvard Kennedy School Gender Action Portal, "Evidence Gendered Wording in Job Advertisements Exists and Sustains Gender Inequality," accessed February 7, 2024, https://gap.hks.harvard.edu/evidence-gendered-wording-job-advertisements-exists-and-sustains-gender-inequality.

pronouns when describing the ideal candidate for open positions. There are also more subtle gender-coded words that can make a difference in the perception of readers. Ads that use masculine-associated wording like "dominant" or "competitive" can discourage women from putting their names in the running, while words like "interpersonal" or "support" may discourage men from submitting applications.

Another stat might help explain this. Employers reportedly only spend six to seven seconds looking at each résumé.[29] (Keep in mind those are just the ones they actually *do* review. Remember our finding that 82 percent of applications get overlooked?) Well, when this is the case, it's unlikely each person is getting a fair chance at landing job opportunities. Here are a few more statistics that suggest a prevalence of bias in the screening process:

- Women are less likely to receive callbacks for interviews.
- Candidates whose names are perceived as Black get fewer callbacks than those whose names are perceived as white.[30]
- Older applicants get 68 percent fewer responses than younger applicants.
- Employers tend to hire candidates with degrees from prestigious schools despite others having more experience.[31]

In-person interviews can be even more problematic. When people meet face-to-face, there's a tendency to judge based on clothing, height,

29 Indeed, "How Long Do Employers Look at Résumés?," accessed February 7, 2024, https://www.indeed.com/career-advice/resumes-cover-letters/how-long-do-employers-look-at-resumes.

30 WBUR, "The Hard Truth about Getting a Job When Your Name Sounds 'Black,'" Here & Now, August 18, 2021, accessed February 7, 2024, https://www.wbur.org/hereandnow/2021/08/18/name-discrimination-jobs.

31 *Harvard Business Review*, "Graduates of Elite Universities Get Paid More. Do They Perform Better?," accessed February 7, 2024, https://hbr.org/2020/09/graduates-of-elite-universities-get-paid-more-do-they-perform-better.

weight, the presence of tattoos, and even the handshake. According to research, an estimated 60 percent of hiring decisions are made within the first fifteen minutes of an interview, and 25 percent are made within only five minutes.[32] These tendencies can extend to video interviews where managers are able to see inside someone's home and hear background noises.

In addition to the simple fact that reducing bias is the right thing to do, it's proven that companies with diverse teams have better retention, productivity, and profitability.[33]

Companies that deploy diversity, equity, and inclusion (DEI) initiatives attract better talent and have better retention. A commitment to diversity and inclusion enhances an organization's reputation as an inclusive and progressive employer. This can attract a wider pool of talent, and once employees are onboarded, an inclusive workplace culture can contribute to higher job satisfaction and retention rates. Seventy-six percent of job seekers said that diversity was important when selecting a job. After the hiring process, employees are 5.4× more likely to stay long term if their workplace is diverse and inclusive.[34] This reduces HR overhead significantly and slashes recruiting and sourcing budgets to strengthen EBITDA.

Additionally, employees tend to perform better and feel more engaged when they work in an environment that values and respects their individual differences. Inclusive workplaces promote a sense of

---

32 Quartz, "Here's How Quickly Interviewers Decide Whether or Not to Hire You," accessed February 7, 2024, https://qz.com/406976/ heres-how-quickly-interviewers-decide-whether-or-not-to-hire-you.

33 University of North Carolina at Pembroke, "Diversity and Inclusion: Good for Business," accessed February 7, 2024, https://online.uncp.edu/degrees/ business/mba/general/diversity-and-inclusion-good-for-business.

34 Great Place to Work, "Why Is Diversity & Inclusion in the Workplace Important?," accessed February 7, 2024, https://www.greatplacetowork.com/ resources/blog/why-is-diversity-inclusion-in-the-workplace-important.

belonging, which can boost morale and productivity. Gender-diverse and inclusive teams outperform gender-homogeneous teams by up to 50 percent, in some cases.[35]

DEI is good for profits and financial goals. Seventy-five percent of companies with frontline decision-making teams that reflect a diverse, inclusive culture exceed their financial goals.[36] Companies in the top quartile for racial/ethnic diversity were 36 percent more likely to achieve higher financial returns, and those in the top quartile for gender diversity were 25 percent more likely to do this.[37]

DEI initiatives don't just enhance the work of the white males. On the contrary, diversity is proven to raise the bar across the board. Diverse companies earn 2.5× higher cash flow per employee than homogeneous teams, are 35 percent more productive, and make better decisions 87 percent of the time, according to McKinsey.

Diversity in the workplace is not only a moral imperative but also a strategic advantage that can contribute to organizational success and sustainability in a rapidly changing world.

Cost of Prioritizing Salaried Workers

Now, think about the consequences of poor work culture at the corporate level or if the white-collar, salaried workforce had turnover rates in the triple digits like the industries that largely rely on hourly workers. Fortune 500 companies would be declaring bankruptcy left

---

35   University of North Carolina at Pembroke, "Diversity and Inclusion."

36   Gartner, "Diversity and Inclusion Build High-Performance Teams," accessed February 7, 2024, https://www.gartner.com/smarterwithgartner/diversity-and-inclusion-build-high-performance-teams.

37   McKinsey & Company, "Diversity Wins: How Inclusion Matters," accessed February 7, 2024, https://www.mckinsey.com/featured-insights/diversity-and-inclusion/diversity-wins-how-inclusion-matters.

and right. So what makes the hiring process better—or at least a little "less broken"—when applied to applicants at the salaried level?

It could be that business owners and managers seem to prioritize hiring these types of workers and putting more effort into recruiting, screening, and interviewing candidates. Of course, they are afforded this amount of extra time because the "click-to-apply" culture doesn't cause the same problems with highly skilled labor. Someone who is trying to hire a VP of marketing with 10+ years of minimum experience at a major corporation is sure to get fewer applicants than a restaurant manager who posts an ad for an entry-level crew member.

They can take the time to give each résumé a thorough review, conduct phone screens, bring candidates in for several rounds of interviews (with multiple managers present), and send a formal job offer after a monthlong hiring process. On the other hand, hourly positions can attract a tremendous number of applications that make it simply unrealistic to properly review and screen each one. And, since many of those applicants apply to 25+ positions at once and often accept the first offer, managers can't spend as much time finding the perfect fit.

However, I don't think the difference in applicant pools should excuse the disparity of managers prioritizing salaried workers in the hiring process. Going back to what I mentioned earlier, these hourly positions aren't largely viewed as long-term careers with room to grow, and people expect turnover. So, when that's the mindset, it creates room for the excuse to simply be, "Well, we just need to hire people as quickly as possible to get fully staffed. It's all right if they aren't the greatest fit since they likely won't be working with us for long, anyway."

Isn't that the lunacy of the situation, though? This type of high-volume sourcing and "speed staffing" without any effort invested into finding the right fit is exactly why hiring managers are stuck in this costly cycle of high turnover in the first place. If they treated hourly applicants with the same level of care in the hiring process, offered good benefits with livable wages, and created pathways for meaningful growth at the company, it would benefit everyone. Employee retention would skyrocket along with cost savings, creating the potential for massive growth in businesses across every industry that employs the hourly workforce.

Also, doesn't it just make sense to want the best possible people working in positions that are typically more customer-facing? Hiring decisions for frontline employees can have dramatic impacts that ripple throughout every facet of the organization, including customer loyalty, public reputation, and profitability. Businesses don't just need all-stars for salaried positions working in offices up on the fifteenth floor. They need top-notch workers interfacing with customers and prospects on the ground floor, maybe even more so. So why are these types of workers still often hired the most carelessly and treated poorly?

Business leaders could be damaging their reputation and hindering their growth potential by trying to fit the same square peg into a round hole in the hiring process for hourly workers and then chalking it up to a series of excuses about the state of the labor market. An honest fiscal analyst would tell them that they ought to prioritize the hiring process for hourly workers and even find a different process that actually works for this workforce's specific needs.

Key Takeaways

Through the story of George, an overworked and underappreciated fast-food employee, we see a microcosm of the broader challenges and opportunities facing businesses that rely heavily on the hourly workforce. This illustrates the real costs and consequences of high turnover and understaffing, emphasizing that the dismissal of hourly workers as easily replaceable can be a costly mistake. The financial cost to replace a worker, when multiplied across all businesses in the country, amounts to an astonishing $1 trillion annually in the United States alone.

Business owners and managers should prioritize hiring in the hourly workforce more and understand the significance of the first ninety days of employment, especially since 20 percent of new hires leave within this period. Improving retention during these crucial first months can drastically reduce turnover costs and boost overall annual retention. They can enhance retention by setting proper expectations, making new hires feel welcome, establishing a comprehensive onboarding plan, scheduling frequent check-ins, and recognizing employee progress.

Furthermore, a positive work environment with a culture that values DEI initiatives not only enhances employee morale but also translates into tangible business benefits such as increased productivity, engagement, and profitability. Conversely, a poor work culture can lead to negative outcomes, including dissatisfied customers and a damaged brand reputation.

Next, we'll explore actionable strategies and tools that businesses can implement to improve the hiring process, including some real-life examples of solutions that major brands have implemented and the results they saw. Hopefully, it will help provide a road map for businesses to navigate the complexities of the hourly workforce and emerge as more resilient, equitable, and successful organizations.

CHAPTER 4

Solutions

Ask, and You Shall Receive

Although I'm a millennial, my parents always taught me to "talk it out." A strong first step to improving the relationship between companies and employers is to simply talk. It's important for your organization to take the needs and values of your employees into account when choosing which benefits or solutions to focus on. Ask them, whether directly or via an anonymous survey, what they care about. Listen to their feedback. Hear them. Then decide. Ultimately, one of the first steps toward truly understanding this workforce and enacting positive change is to engage with them. See them.

Wages

People say "money isn't everything" all the time, but for the vast majority of the hourly workforce, money means a lot. And it's no surprise that hourly workers voice a need for higher wages to manage inflation in other aspects of their lives.

One study found that half of hourly workers are not confident they'll be able to retire comfortably, which would naturally weigh heavily on anyone's mind and make it hard to find motivation each day.[38] Another survey found a wealth of insight into the effects of financial challenges on hourly workers, including:

- 93 percent of all hourly workers find managing their finances stressful.
- 71 percent report this stress has a negative impact on their mental or physical health.
- 79 percent of Gen Z hourly workers don't always have enough money to pay bills on time.[39]

As an example, a fast-food cook makes an average of $13.43 per hour, cashiers earn an average of $13.81 per hour ($13.10 for gas station cashiers), and hotel housekeeping staff members earn $15.35 per hour.

---

38 CBS News Minnesota, "Half of Hourly Workers Not Confident They'll Retire Comfortably, Survey Shows," accessed February 7, 2024, https://www.cbsnews.com/minnesota/news/half-of-hourly-workers-not-confident-theyll-retire-comfortably-survey-shows/.

39 PR Newswire, "3 out of 4 Gen Z Hourly Workers Say the Stress of Managing Their Finances Has a Negative Impact on Their Health," accessed February 7, 2024, https://www.prnewswire.com/news-releases/3-out-of-4-gen-z-hourly-workers-say-the-stress-of-managing-their-finances-has-a-negative-impact-on-their-health-301890434.html.

For these workers, their hourly wage adds up to $27,920 per year if they work full-time hours year-round. That number, also taken from 2022, is only a couple hundred dollars higher than the Federal Poverty Line for a family of four in 2022.[40]

However, due to various factors like legislation, cultural pressures, and the need to attract more workers, hourly wages are experiencing an upward trend. Here's a snapshot of the increase over time in the leisure and hospitality industries:[41]

Hourly Wage Growth
Cumulative percent change in average hourly earnings from January 2021

—— Total Private   – – Leisure and Hospitality

Chart: Andy Kiersz/Insider

Source: Insider calculations with data from Bureau of Labor Statistics via FRED

It's important to note that although wages are increasing, the federal minimum wage is still $7.25. This has remained stagnant since 2009. However, twenty-five states recently passed bills to increase

---

40   Healthcare.gov, "Federal Poverty Level (FPL)," accessed February 7, 2024, https://www.healthcare.gov/glossary/federal-poverty-level-fpl/.

41   Business Insider, "Why Is Every Place Asking for Tips, but not to Pay Workers More?," accessed February 7, 2024, https://www.businessinsider.com/why-is-every-place-asking-for-tips-pay-workers-more-2023-5.

their minimum wages, with a few states that now have elected to increase those minimums above $15 per hour:

- Massachusetts
- New Jersey
- Connecticut
- California
- Maryland

Raising wages is not a feasible option or the best possible strategy for every single business. But employers should operate under the assumption that wages, particularly in this workforce, are absolutely top of mind for workers. Pay ought to be discussed regularly as a leadership team and seen as a tool for recruitment and retention just as other solutions outlined in this book.

Financial Empowerment

Have you thought about including the option for customers to tip employees in your digital payment technology?

While this has caught some people off guard who are prompted to add an optional tip at establishments that didn't used to have this option, brands like Starbucks and Chipotle have been testing it out. It can help with employee compensation and even incentivize workers to deliver top-class service. However, keep in mind that it could lead to customer dissatisfaction among those who feel it's a ploy by companies to help cover the rising cost of their employees. (I suppose they're not wrong....)[42]

---

42   Ibid.

This next financial benefit I'll mention here is a bit tricky. It's the idea of a 401(k). While it might seem straightforward, and plenty of businesses offer them as options to employees, these programs must be done right to work in the hourly workforce. Remember, we're talking about a group of people who live paycheck to paycheck, sometimes relying on personal loans to pay bills in certain circumstances. Do you think many of them would be able to dedicate a portion of their paycheck to a 401(k) fund? If you do decide to try a 401(k) program for employees, I suggest having your company match contributions to make it financially worthwhile. Otherwise, you might see that nobody opts into it.

Employees also tend to be more engaged at work when they benefit from the success of the company. I reward my employees with equity ownership at Sprockets, as many other business leaders do at their companies. Financial incentives like employee stock options (ESOs) at discounted rates can motivate workers in a way that standard pay doesn't. Some people take their wages as a given. They know that as long as they come to work each day and do at least the bare minimum, they'll get a consistent paycheck.

Stock options can inspire them to go above and beyond for the good of the company as well as their own bank account. Of course, just like with a 401(k), it might not be feasible for some hourly workers to afford stocks, even with the employee discount program. But if you make the program more financially attainable, they might stick around longer to see the company grow along with the value of their shares, especially when their ESOs have vesting dates over time.

Speaking of sticking around longer, you could include retention bonuses as part of a compensation package to help reduce turnover. For example, you could offer employees a $500 bonus once they make it to the ninety-day mark, which is a common benchmark for hiring success in the hourly workforce. Then, you might give them another $1,000 for every six months after that.

Of course, I'm just throwing out numbers here. The exact amount is completely up to you based on what your business can afford and what you believe will keep people around. Just make sure to outline it clearly in your employee handbook so there's no confusion down the line.

Innovative Financial Solution

A particularly popular benefit that's been on the rise recently is offering daily pay to employees. And while you might think that processing payroll for all your workers every day would be too tedious and time-consuming, there are on-demand pay and earned-wage solutions that make it easy. There are often no major changes to your payroll process or extra paperwork to complete.

Employees get access to their earned wages in real time to ease financial stress and adapt to any unforeseen circumstances with bills while you save money on turnover costs and keep workers longer. Just keep in mind that employees may have to pay fees to get their money early, which can add up, but you can opt to cover the cost to make it an even more attractive benefit for job seekers.

Growth and Development Opportunities

When you invest in the growth and development of your employees, showing them you truly care about their livelihood, they'll usually return the favor. As the famous Sir Richard Branson said, "Train people well enough so they can leave, treat them well enough so they don't want to."

A common benefit that would fall into this category is a tuition reimbursement program. Whether your company covers all of it or a percentage, or helps cover the cost of books, it can be greatly appreciated by workers. And it's not just appealing to younger workers who are graduating high school and about to head off to college. There are plenty of older employees in the hourly workforce who would love to go back to school to get their GED, earn a bachelor's degree, or get a master's degree. You'd help them better themselves and gain access to more opportunities than a large majority of the hourly workforce is usually afforded. And who knows, they might turn into long-term employees with the right career pathways available. It doesn't hurt to promote someone from within who knows the company inside and out rather than take a risk on an external hire who might require extensive training and not work out.

If your employees aren't interested in traditional schooling, or it's just not affordable, that's all right. There are plenty of other ways to help them grow as people and professionals. For instance, you could pay for them to complete certification programs that help them land higher-paying jobs. Amazon is one example of a company that has done this with its "Upskilling 2025 Pledge."[43] Through this program, they're giving frontline employees access to ten different programs to build their skill sets. This type of benefit isn't exclusive to Amazon employees, though. For instance, if you own a fast-food restaurant or retail store, you could help workers obtain their SHRM Certified Professional (SHRM-CP) certification so they can transition to more HR-related roles at your company.

You can also look for ways to improve your existing internal training process. This can take the form of allowing new hires to

---

43 Amazon, "Our Upskilling 2025 Programs," accessed February 7, 2024, https://www.aboutamazon.com/news/workplace/our-upskilling-2025-programs.

complete training online in the comfort of their home before their first day. It can also extend beyond their initial onboarding so they get continuous on-the-job training to help them learn new skills. These can be training programs to help them excel at their current job in addition to those that would aid them in ascending the ranks at your company.

Several franchisees today actually started out as hourly workers in entry-level positions at their brand, and I'm sure many of you reading this book fall into this category. I found an interesting stat that 95 percent of Dominos' franchisees were once delivery drivers or part-time employees.[44] Basically, "If you build it, they will come." Set up clear career pathways and provide the necessary training to give your workers the opportunity to become managers, own their own locations, and even become full-fledged franchises of their own. If you are, in fact, one of the business leaders who started out in an entry-level role, why not return the favor by mentoring employees who are in the position you were once in?

Now, mentorship programs and one-on-one training initiatives are great but don't make the mistake of thinking that workplace learning is a one-way street. Sure, the "higher-ups" with more experience can help teach newer employees how to perform their jobs well and guide them toward achieving their career goals. However, business owners and supervisors can often learn from the frontline crew members.

Take a moment to consider the value frontline employees can provide from their unique perspectives. We're siloed as decision-makers in the boardroom, but hourly workers likely have great insights that can add a ton of efficiencies. I always think about the scene in *The Office* when Darryl impresses the new CEO, Jo, with an innova-

---

44 Entrepreneur, "Transforming In-House Talent into Business Owners," accessed February 7, 2024, https://www.entrepreneur.com/franchises/transforming-in-house-talent-into-business-owners/466040.

tive way to ship packages more efficiently. He then came up with the idea to have delivery drivers sell paper themselves and gain company incentives in return. It's a great idea that is foolishly brushed aside by Michael but is, of course, implemented once Jo loves this idea as well.

Jo quickly saw his potential and moved him up to the main office floor while Michael was selfishly holding Darryl back from moving up the ladder and providing tremendous value to the company, possibly in part due to Michael overlooking him as just another warehouse worker. Of course, this is another fictional representation, but I think it's one we can learn from.

Make sure you always ask for feedback and insights from those you might be inadvertently overlooking. They could have ideas that significantly improve operations because, well, they're the ones who are actually performing the tasks each day. Plus, they could continue to provide even more value as excellent internal hires for management positions with their experience.

There's one more "growth and development" type of benefit I'd like to mention here because it can be particularly impactful for the hourly workforce. I don't know about you, but personal finance wasn't required at my high school. It turns out that only fifteen states require high school students to study personal finance, which is particularly shocking since the average American has $96,371 in debt.[45] Something doesn't add up.

While people can point to a variety of different reasons for this issue, you can be part of the solution by offering financial literacy programs. It can be a course within your company's LMS. Or, you can set up regularly scheduled seminars that employees can attend.

---

45 National Debt Relief, "Financial Education Not Part of Ccurriculum," accessed February 7, 2024, https://www.nationaldebtrelief.com/blog/financial-wellness/financial-education/financial-education-not-part-of-curriculum/.

It can even be as simple as making sure each person has access to a reliable financial advisor. Whatever form it takes, a program like this can make a positive impact on the lives of hourly workers who struggle financially and don't see much hope for a comfortable retirement.

Innovative Growth and Development Solution

While we covered the topic of training already, there's a training solution that's completely transforming how some companies get their employees ready for work. Virtual training can be a unique way to help new hires prior to their first day, as well as current employees, level up their skill set. Now, many people think of virtual training as a video meeting where an instructor or manager talks to you in real time, which is accurate.

However, there are solutions that take the definition to a whole new level with virtual reality training. While this isn't anything particularly new, there have been significant technological advances to make it increasingly popular. VR is being used to teach people how to navigate dangerous situations that could potentially happen at work, especially for pilots, firefighters, and surgeons.

However, there are potentially unlimited applications, even in the hourly workforce. It can be used to help people improve their soft skills, like leadership for management positions, and learning through VR is linked to faster training time and higher levels of confidence with new skills.[46]

---

46 PwC, "Virtual Reality Study," accessed February 7, 2024, https://www.pwc.com/us/en/tech-effect/emerging-tech/virtual-reality-study.html.

Health and Wellness Programs

In the white-collar, salaried workforce, we often take PTO for granted. Sure, we might stress over asking our bosses to use our days off around the holidays or worry about what our inbox might look like when we come back to work, but the option is always there for paid time off. Emphasis on "paid."

Hourly workers don't have that privilege, even though many of them work the same amount of time as salaried employees. If they want to take a day off, they lose a day's worth of pay. And if they want to take a vacation, say goodbye to a paycheck entirely. Workers can typically accrue one hour of sick time per thirty hours worked, but even then, it's not guaranteed to be *paid* sick time.[47] If you were living paycheck to paycheck and came down with the flu, would you take an unpaid sick day and risk not being able to pay bills on time, or would you try to tough it out and still go to work? I think we all know the answer, and it isn't the ideal situation for anyone.

Now, let's say it isn't the flu. What if they were in a car accident and suffered serious injuries? Hourly workers don't always get access to healthcare at an affordable cost through their employer. They might get vision and dental benefits after an initial probationary period, but health insurance can be much more expensive, which makes it less common. So, they often must battle with the idea of paying for expensive coverage in the marketplace or opting not to have any health insurance.

Now that person who may have been working for you for months, maybe even years, without being late or missing a single day can't

47   Center for American Progress, "The State of Paid Sick Time in the U.S. in 2023," accessed February 7, 2024, https://www.americanprogress.org/article/the-state-of-paid-sick-time-in-the-u-s-in-2023/.

work for a while. Let's say six months. Do you think most companies would give them job security for when they can return to work, or would they quickly hire someone else to keep their business afloat? What would *you* do? In an ideal world, this wouldn't be an issue at all since the invisible workforce would get the benefits they deserve, especially health insurance—something every hardworking human deserves. However, people in this scenario end up injured, jobless, and drowning in hospital bills.

Have you ever thought about offering childcare services or support to your employees? Sixty-two percent of parents in the United States struggle to find childcare so they can support themselves and their families.[48] Additionally, 83 percent of millennials say they would leave a job for one that provided more family-friendly services like childcare. This employee benefit program is often overlooked or forgotten by employers, so if you have the resources to do so, it will make many parents happy. Plus, childcare services can boost employee recruitment, retention, and attendance.[49] Another win-win.

You can also encourage your hourly workers to maintain a healthy lifestyle by offering gym membership discounts. Regular exercise can boost employee engagement and productivity.[50] The healthier your hourly workers are, the more likely they will come to work energized and ready to conquer the day. Maintaining a healthy lifestyle can even

---

48 Learning Care Group, "Employer Solutions," accessed February 7, 2024, https://www.learningcaregroup.com/employer-solutions/.

49 St. Louis Business Journal, "Lessons from the Pandemic: Companies Offering Child Care Assistance May See Improved Retention," accessed February 7, 2024, https://www.bizjournals.com/stlouis/news/2021/02/04/lessons-from-the-pandemic-companies-offering-chil.html.

50 Society for Human Resource Management (SHRM), "Fitting in Fitness on Company Time," accessed February 7, 2024, https://www.shrm.org/resourcesandtools/legal-and-compliance/state-and-local-updates/pages/fitting-in-fitness-on-company-time.aspx.

help reduce absenteeism. When people exercise often, it strengthens their immune system to protect against pathogens and even reduces their risk for major health issues like diabetes, heart disease, and cancer.[51] That's an initiative I'm sure we can all get behind.

Now, let's talk turkey. And by that, I literally mean food. When you're out eating with your family at a restaurant and see all the restaurant employees rushing around and serving customers, do you think they get a chance to get a dish for themselves? Not always. They might work in a food establishment, but it would be wrong to assume they get a chance to eat a decent meal, let alone a quick snack.

While some companies offer excellent free-meal programs, there are others that don't execute such programs properly. There are a variety of reasons, some obvious and some not. Restaurants might provide free or discounted food to workers during their breaks, but what if they're so understaffed and busy they don't get a chance to relax and eat properly? Plus, think of any food—even your absolute favorite dish. Do you think you could eat the same thing every day without getting tired of it while you spend hours upon hours cooking, smelling, and serving it? Naturally, we desire variety.

This is all to say employees should be given free meals during shifts, with the proper amount of time to relax and eat, a variety of options to enjoy, and maybe even get some sort of "food credit" to order delivery from somewhere other than where they work. It's good for the health and happiness of employees, and I can't imagine business owners want a bunch of "hangry" employees serving customers every day.

---

51   National Center for Biotechnology Information, "PMCID: PMC6523821," accessed February 7, 2024, https://www.ncbi.nlm.nih.gov/pmc/articles/ PMC6523821/.

Innovative Health and Wellness Solution

Now, let's say it isn't what some consider "physical health" at all, although there's plenty of research showing it has direct impacts on physical health. Mental health has been a topic that's been unfortunately buried and ignored, much like the invisible workforce, but should be prioritized as well. Fortunately, we've seen great strides in society in recent years to address mental health issues and destigmatize the idea of getting help, but there's always room for more progress.

You can help by supplementing your health insurance package with an Employee Assistance Program (EAP). These give workers easy access to confidential counseling and resources for anxiety, depression, substance abuse, grief, and trauma. The list goes on, and much of the help can be accessed virtually from the comfort of their homes. If you're worried about cost, EAPs are largely affordable at just seventy-five cents to two dollars per member and typically have a good ROI, in addition to the obvious benefits of providing support to people in need.[52] Research shows that for each dollar spent on an EAP, employers save five to sixteen dollars through reduced absenteeism, accidents, work grievances, and more.[53] And you can select or customize an EAP to fit the needs of your employees.

---

52   Society for Human Resource Management (SHRM), "Companies Seek to Boost Low Usage of Employee Assistance Programs," accessed February 7, 2024, https://www.shrm.org/topics-tools/news/hr-magazine/companies-seek-to-boost-low-usage-employee-assistance-programs.

53   BambooHR, "Employee Assistance Programs: A Comprehensive Guide," accessed February 7, 2024, https://www.bamboohr.com/blog/employee-assistance-programs.

Diversity, Equity, and Inclusion Efforts

As discussed earlier, it's far too easy for bias to creep into every stage of the hiring process, whether consciously or unconsciously. So, one of the first steps toward improving DEI in your organization is to nip bias in the bud. It must be a priority for every business leader to prevent bias from happening in the first place when applicants are screened and selected.

It's important to note that there's no "silver bullet" to eliminate the issue completely. Even with the following solutions, and no matter how good-hearted the effort is, there's no guarantee bias won't still affect hiring decisions. However, I remain optimistic that we can collectively work toward at least removing as much bias as possible. It will take some time and significant effort from business leaders, but it's absolutely worthwhile. Otherwise, millions of people will continue to face unfair barriers to employment—barriers that have been built over time and need to be dismantled.

With that being said, start by providing training for managers on fair hiring practices. Whether they realize it or not, managers may be building a homogeneous applicant pool by using gender-coded words in job descriptions that attract one gender over others or unfairly eliminating candidates by asking interview questions that introduce bias (including some that are even illegal). The list can go on.

There are plenty of online training courses and certifications available. Better yet, DEI consultants can be exceptional resources for employee training and various other services. They can audit current practices, identify areas for improvement, offer diversity training, and help ensure compliance with laws and regulations. It's also a good idea to consult an expert when implementing new DEI programs.

Make sure training isn't just a one-time thing, though. It should be an ongoing process to ensure your organization stays on track toward DEI goals and that people don't revert to unfair practices. Plus, consider all the turnover in industries that employ hourly workers. It's not just crew members; manager turnover is significant as well. And when you're constantly hiring new managers, how can you be sure they adhere to fair practices and DEI initiatives? Consistent, ongoing training. While DEI consultants are fantastic, consider hiring for a role like chief diversity officer on a permanent basis. It can be their sole responsibility to make sure your company improves and continues to uphold diversity standards.

Keep in mind that DEI efforts aren't just about ethnicity, though. You need to put measures in place so that LGBTQ+ individuals are treated fairly and aren't discriminated against during the hiring process and during employment. Conducting training and hiring a chief diversity officer can both help with this, but here are a few more ways to show your company's commitment to diversity of all kinds. For instance, you can donate to LGBTQ+ organizations that provide resources for the LGBTQ+ community. Here are a few reputable ones: Parents, Families, and Friends of Lesbians and Gays (PFLAG); Services and Advocacy for LGBT Elders (SAGE); The Trevor Project; and the Human Rights Campaign.

No matter the monetary amount, donations directly and positively impact these individuals' lives. Regardless of which organization you choose, be sure to do your research. Encourage your employees to support your chosen organization as well. You could even consider getting your employees involved by having a small fundraiser.

Another LGBTQ+ initiative you could implement is adding pronouns to name tags and email signatures. Addressing someone by their desired pronouns is a basic form of respect that everyone—

regardless of sexuality or gender identity—deserves. Some top brands now offer employees name tags with pronouns to be more inclusive of all genders. This eliminates confusion and misunderstanding, especially for non-gender-conforming individuals who are more likely to be misgendered. It's easy for these folks to feel singled out, so by adding your pronouns to your name tag, you are actively showing your support for the LGBTQ+ community and normalizing the conversation around gender identity.

Also, take the time to redefine how you and your employees address customers. For example, instead of greeting customers with "Hey, guys!" your associates could say "Hey, everyone," "Hey, folks," or even "Hey, y'all." Small, simple changes like these foster inclusivity. Plus, it signals that your location(s) are welcoming toward all individuals. Remember, it can be uncomfortable for nonbinary, transgender, intersex, and other LGBTQ+ folks to speak up, especially if they are misgendered. You can be proactive about the change and make a positive difference without an issue occurring that spurs you to finally take action.

Innovative DEI Solution

There are plenty of excellent training courses, certification programs, and DEI experts to help guide you in the right direction. And while I don't want to take any attention away from those, I think it's important to mention there are tech-based solutions as well. There are HR tech platforms that reduce bias and contribute to a more equitable workplace, and there's no reason why you can't implement both types of solutions.

For example, there are equitable hiring tools and platforms that essentially "scrub" the information on applications that could elicit unconscious bias from managers. They can hide details such as names, addresses, ages, and the schools they attended so the playing field is more or less "equal" for all candidates. Hiring managers can then focus on what truly matters, like the important skills and personality traits needed to be successful in the role. This is commonly called "blind hiring," which can be done without tech to a certain degree.

This practice originated when orchestras in 2000 had musicians audition from behind a curtain. However, today's software that automatically strips details from résumés and applications makes it much easier. It's not a 100 percent fault-proof silver bullet, but it can be a step in the right direction. And, if your organization has a solid grasp on equitable résumé screening practices with a consistently diverse applicant pool, your efforts might be better focused elsewhere, like in the interview process. This is just one of many examples to advance DEI.

Company Culture Initiatives

Tech companies and software start-ups have their beer and ping-pong tables, but what do hourly workers have? I'm sure you can assume that's a rhetorical question. The point is that the hourly workforce is so "invisible" that they fly under the radar of any potential culture discussions.

Some might think with the high turnover rate, there's no ROI in trying to implement any culture or engagement initiatives. What if we just started with learning the names of our frontline workers who represent our companies every day? Going back to the story I shared in the introduction to this book, I believe there's so much untapped potential in simply learning the names of every Danny at companies. It has ripple effects on the individual's life and the company's success.

For example, have you ever been annoyed by a teacher who never cared to learn your name in class? Point proven. That should be the baseline. Here are additional steps owners and managers should take to improve company culture in their workforce.

This should be easy to implement, and it might even be a stretch to include it under "benefits," although you could make it a standard part of your benefits package. Consider scheduling regular happy hours for employees. It could be once a week, once a month, or even quarterly. No matter how you set up the happy hours, it's a great way for managers and crew members to socialize in a casual setting outside of work. If the white-collar, salaried workforce can do it, why not the hourly workforce? Of course, try to be flexible when setting up the schedule since many hourly workers have multiple jobs. They might also lack easy access to transportation, but you can use that as an opportunity to go the extra mile by providing Ubers or offering them a ride yourself.

Employee recognition is another simple yet significant "benefit" to focus on at your company. While owners and managers should always recognize employees for their work, it should go beyond a high-five or "nice job." Think about creative ways to thank your team for their contribution to the success of the business. You can start doing Employee of the Month and highlight their hard work at company meetings. It could come with an incentive like a free day of PTO, a gift card, a cash bonus on their next paycheck, or even something like lunch with the CEO. While the classic Wall of Fame is nice, not everyone wants their picture plastered up at work, and I think we can all admit we'd prefer a cash bonus.

Innovative Company Culture Solution

Plenty of employee recognition platforms nowadays make it easier than ever to highlight top performers and automate the sending of gifts or company swag. Some of the platforms give you your own internal "social media platform" where team members can highlight each other's contributions with pictures and fun messages. It builds a sense of community and camaraderie that so many workplaces lack.

Many programs like this also come with a comprehensive catalog of rewards that employees can choose from, often receiving items like gift cards instantly. They get to choose exactly what they want, rather than the employer guessing what they'd like best. Some employee recognition programs also enable you to set up goals or fun challenges employees can participate in to win rewards. They can be health and wellness challenges, completely independent from business goals. It's a great way to keep motivation and engagement up while encouraging employees to care for themselves outside of work.

Recruiting Solutions

Rewind for a second. All of these benefits and solutions I've discussed are great for humanizing the hourly workers starting on day one of their new jobs, but they should start so much earlier. The hiring process is equally important, if not more, for bringing respect and dignity to the invisible workforce. As I mentioned earlier, it's really where the experience begins for hourly workers. It should be a positive applicant journey from start to finish and launch their employment on the right foot. So, here are a few ways you can make that a reality.

First, let's face it: Gen Zers and millennials make up a massive portion of the hourly workforce, and they've grown up with social media. Business owners and operators should embrace social media as a recruiting strategy to reach their audience where they are. It's all right if you're not tech-savvy because I'll help explain everything you need to know to recruit the right workers on social media platforms.

Second, know your needs. Before you start messaging all your social media followers with private messages about how great your job opportunities are, take a moment and assess the situation. What job openings do you have? Where are you in the hiring process? Are you looking for someone to create their own position? What skill sets would you like a potential employee to possess? What is your company culture like, and what personality traits would enable a candidate to mesh well with the current team?

Defining your purpose in hiring will give you an ample idea of who you are seeking and what that person must bring to the table. If you are adamant about sending private messages for social recruiting, look through your top commenters. What kinds of engagement do they offer? Are they helpful to other customers? Do they care about your brand as you do? What types of hobbies do they have, according to the content they post? Learn about the content your consumers engage with. If someone seems like a good fit from there, reach out.

Third, get creative. If you plan to use social media for recruiting Gen Zers and millennials, then you need to create content that will resonate and inspire them to act. Creating and sharing blog posts that answer niche questions can be particularly effective for engaging people in your target demographic. You can also create posts on various social media platforms, such as Facebook and LinkedIn, asking fun questions that would capture the interest of your audience.

There doesn't need to be an actual correct answer to your question; simply seeing how people's minds work is a great way to identify high-quality candidates. Just don't forget about Instagram, especially when it comes to Gen Zers and millennials. Consider holding a photo contest. Encourage your followers to come up with a unique photo and creative tagline related to your business. Make sure you ask all participants to tag your business account and use a particular hashtag. You can give as many or as few details as you want. While you won't be able to legally use the results in your marketing—unless you onboard the winner—you will get a great look at your talent pool.

Fourth, be consistent. To effectively execute a social media recruitment strategy, it's essential to maintain a consistent presence online with your company's accounts. This tells people that you're easy to reach, you'll respond in a timely manner, and you value a strong work ethic.

Consider scheduling several posts at once that will be published on a regular, weekly timeline to make things easier for yourself. Pay particular attention to your audience insights on each social media platform so that your posts go live at ideal times to reach your target demographic. You can even come up with a simple social media calendar to plan posts more effectively.

Using a wide range of media is also fantastic for reaching different people. Some individuals are visual learners who love infographics. Others are audio learners, so podcasts are great. Utilize a variety of media to engage your followers on multiple platforms, allowing them the luxury to choose when, how, and what they want to learn.

Fifth, choose the right channels. Every social media platform reaches different demographics and has different innate purposes. LinkedIn is an excellent platform for recruiting and job seekers. Here, you'll find candidates actively looking for work and passive candidates willing to take a better offer. Instagram is typically where millennials and Gen Zers go to check out more visual, fun messages. X (formerly known as Twitter) is mainly about news headlines and trending hashtags. This is a fantastic place for your polls and quippy questions. Lastly, Facebook has become the world's largest address book. You can find almost everyone on Facebook (but don't expect Gen Zers to spend much time scrolling through their feeds—they're more inclined to be on Instagram).

Simply put, knowing what each social media site is designed for helps you maximize marketing efforts for your job opportunity. Ultimately, recruiting online takes research, just like any other form of marketing. However, social media is meant to be fun and relaxing. Enjoy the questions you ask and the comments you interact with. At the end of the day, you want to mesh well with your next hire.

Sixth, create effective job postings to have a successful recruiting strategy. According to an Indeed survey, 52 percent of job seekers said the quality of the description was very or extremely influential in their decision to apply or not.[54] And by "quality," that didn't just include whether or not it was written well. They also looked at formatting, typos, and grammatical mistakes. So don't rush through it. It should also include all key details that job seekers need to know to feel confident clicking "apply" but not be too long that they don't bother reading it all. Try to keep it between 100 and 300 words (these shorter posts get 8.4 percent more applications per views[55]) while including job title, pay range, responsibilities, requirements, work environment, company values, and how to apply.

Some people might be hesitant to include the wage information in job postings, but it's pretty important and will continue to be. That same Indeed survey I mentioned earlier found that nearly one in four

---

54 Indeed, "How to Improve Your Job Postings to Attract Better Candidates," accessed February 7, 2024, https://www.indeed.com/hire/c/info/how-to-improve-your-job-postings-to-attract-better-candidates.

55 LinkedIn Talent Solutions, "New Job Post Stats," accessed February 7, 2024, https://www.linkedin.com/business/talent/blog/talent-acquisition/new-job-post-stats.

job seekers said that compensation info was the most important part of a job description. At the very least, include a potential pay range for them to reference. Also, make sure your description doesn't include any "gender-coded" language.[56] For example, ads that use masculine-associated wording like "dominant" or "competitive" can discourage women from applying, while words like "interpersonal" or "support" may discourage men. I have one more bonus tip for you when it comes to the job description: Consider asking someone in the position currently to assist with writing or reviewing it. They can be a great resource to ensure you accurately describe the role and responsibilities.

Seventh, think about the messaging for what you should send applicants, whether you decide to move forward with them in the hiring process or not. Communication with hourly workers is important, even when you ultimately must tell them no. After all, how can we build a culture of mutual respect if we ghost applicants instead of being forthright with them? So, don't just send a plain, boring email telling them when to come in for an interview and then not send the others anything at all.

Try something along the lines of, "Congrats, [Name]! We've reviewed your application and would love to learn more about you with an interview. You'll be meeting with our hiring manager, Tim. What are some times you're available next week? Looking forward to our chat!" For the applicants you choose not to interview, pretty much anything is better than nothing (within reason). You could send them an email saying, "Hi [Name], Thank you for your interest in the position, but we've decided to move forward with another candidate

56 Harvard Kennedy School Gender Action Portal, "Evidence Gendered Wording in Job Advertisements Exists and Sustains Gender Inequality," accessed February 7, 2024, https://gap.hks.harvard.edu/evidence-gendered-wording-job-advertisements-exists-and-sustains-gender-inequality.

at this time. However, we will keep your application on file and keep you posted about any future opportunities you'd be a good fit for. Thanks again!" And that part should be true. You never know when you'll need applicants suddenly for another opening. It's better to keep a community of interested applicants rather than burn bridges if you can help it.

Innovative Recruitment Solution

Remember when I mentioned you need to avoid "gender-coded" words in your job descriptions? It's OK if you aren't familiar with the term, but it *is* important you now learn about it and actively take steps to remove them from all current and future job listings. Fortunately, there are tools available online that can help you identify and remove language like this from your descriptions. They make it easy by allowing you to copy and paste your content.

You can then see if the overall text is coded one way or another, see which words are problematic, and edit from there. There are also lists of masculine-coded words and feminine-coded words that you can read through or keep up on your computer screen to reference while writing your next job description.

Employee Selection Solutions

Interview time.

Start by picking a time that is convenient for both the interviewer and the interviewee. Don't simply give them one option for a time they must work into their schedule. Then, figure out where you'll be conducting the interview. If it's in a tattered booth at the back corner of a restaurant, that definitely sets a bad tone.

Make it known that you care and have put effort into the interview. A candidate should feel welcomed and comfortable from the moment they walk in the door. Say hello, offer them a drink, especially if they must wait, and ask purposeful questions that help you get to know them as a potential employee as well as a person. It should be a two-way conversation. Leave room for pauses to ask if they have any questions, and make it clear you really want them to ask questions. It could help by having a member of the actual crew come over during the interview and answer any questions they have. Remember, people are prone to anxiety in these situations and don't have the luxury of taking questions "offline." Talking to someone on the team with a friendly, bubbly personality can help put them at ease and explain what working there is really like.

You can also supplement or straight-up replace the interview stage with a preemployment assessment. Preemployment assessments are tools used in the prescreening step of the hiring process to predict an applicant's likelihood of success. While there are several different types of tests, preemployment assessments provide employers with details about their applicants to help them make smarter hiring decisions. It's a sneak peek into how applicants will behave and perform in the workplace. There are several different types of assessments you can use.

- Job Knowledge Tests: Applicants are asked to demonstrate their expertise on processes they'll encounter if they were to be hired.
- Integrity Tests: These questions evaluate an applicant's reliability and honesty. Candidates may also be required to pass a drug test.
- Cognitive Ability Tests: The most common preemployment assessment measures a candidate's mental capacity to

think through complex situations they may encounter at the workplace.[57]

- Personality Tests: Analyze personality traits to determine whether or not an applicant will fit in with the company culture and be an engaged, productive employee.
- Emotional Intelligence Tests: Gauge how a candidate builds relationships and resolves conflict, especially in high-pressure situations.
- Skills Assessment Tests: Evaluate an applicant's soft and hard skills.
- Physical Ability Tests: Assess a candidate's physical strength, such as lifting fifty pounds.

Naturally, some business owners have questions about the legality or ethics involved with assessment tools. The simple answer is yes, preemployment assessments are legal on a federal, state, and local level in the United States as long as they are Equal Employment Opportunity Commission (EEOC) compliant.[58] There are a few laws in place to eliminate discrimination "against anyone on the basis of personal qualities that aren't job-related," including:

- Title VII of the Civil Rights Act of 1964: Prohibits failure to hire an individual based on race, gender, color, religion, or national origin.

---

57   Society for Human Resource Management (SHRM), "Screening by Means of Pre-Employment Testing," accessed February 7, 2024, https://www.shrm.org/resourcesandtools/tools-and-samples/toolkits/pages/screeningbymeansofpreemploymenttesting.aspx.

58   PSI Services LLC, "Is Pre-Employment Testing Legal?," accessed February 7, 2024, https://www.psionline.com/wp-content/uploads/Is-Pre-Employment-Testing-Legal_PSI.pdf.

- Age Discrimination in Employment Act of 1967: It is illegal for employers to discriminate against people forty and older.
- Americans with Disabilities Act of 1990: Employers cannot discriminate against anyone with any disability.

It's also important employers understand the validity of preemployment assessments used in their hiring process. There are currently three primary forms of validity approved by the EEOC:

- Construct Validity: Whether a questionnaire measures what it claims to measure and in a way that is consistent with the definition of those dimensions.
- Criterion-Related Validity: Shows that the dimensions or scales are predictive of something tangible such as differences in scores on a scale related to work behavior or performance.
- Content Validity: Demonstrates that the behaviors measured in the selection procedure are a representative sample of the behaviors of the job in question.

Here's some additional information about the pros and cons of preemployment assessments to help you decide if you'd like to integrate one into your hiring system and what to keep an eye out for when selecting one:

Pros:

- Accelerates the Hiring Process: Employers can make smarter, more informed decisions about who they hire, therefore reducing costly employee turnover.
- Increases Quality of Hires: When an applicant is willing to take a preemployment assessment, it shows they are committed and are likely more interested in the position than an applicant who fails to complete a test.

- Provides Equal Opportunity: Every applicant will take the same preemployment assessment, ensuring a fair and honest process.

Cons:

- Partial Picture of the Candidate: Like résumés, some preemployment assessments only provide a snapshot of an applicant's character. It's important to consider other factors and refrain from solely basing your decision to move an applicant forward in the hiring process based on these tests.
- Questionable Validity: Unfortunately, not all preemployment assessments are accurate and truthful; some can have an adverse impact when used in the hiring process.

Some people also wonder if it's worth it since it adds another step to the hiring process, which might increase applicant drop-off. However, I still believe preemployment assessments are worth it by helping you narrow down which candidates you want to spend time interviewing. Just make sure you choose one that is brief and maintains a smooth application process for people. As long as it only takes a few extra minutes, it's worthwhile to potentially save you thousands of dollars, hours of time in your workday, and one heck of a hiring headache. Plus, it can help ensure the candidate will have a positive experience at work by determining whether or not they are the right fit for the company and position.

Now, when you reach the point where you've decided who to hire, use this as an opportunity to start their official relationship with the company on a high note. Don't just send a basic email with a contract attached. Think about what you can do to make it feel like a special moment for them. After all, it is. I'm not saying you need to throw them a party or send an edible arrangement, but simply picking up the phone and calling the person to offer them the job can make a difference.

Mention your excitement to have them as part of the team, ask if they have any questions again, and explain the next steps if they accept the offer. It should be something you both feel good about. You're not just filling an open role. You're giving a new opportunity to a human being—someone who may desperately need the paycheck and is genuinely excited to work for you.

Innovative Employee Selection Solution

Basically, any initiative to improve the hiring process is a step in the right direction to humanize and highlight the invisible workforce for powering your business. Sprockets can help too. It's a unique solution that automatically identifies the ideal applicants based on shared personality traits with a company's current top performers.

There's no need to rely on guesswork or gut feelings—just proven science rooted in psycholinguistics. It works perfectly alongside any current system and asks applicants three simple questions. The AI-powered matching system then instantly sees who has the key personality traits for success and synergy at each location. Ultimately, you end up with a team of top performers who get along and stay long term, improving workplace culture and saving you thousands of dollars in employee turnover costs.

Key Takeaways

There are various strategies and practices that businesses can implement to address the challenges faced by the hourly workforce. The first step is to acknowledge the financial hardships prevalent among hourly workers, with many living paycheck to paycheck and struggling with financial insecurity, and then explore how you can enhance your practices to foster a more supportive and equitable work environment.

In addressing business practices, it's important to take a holistic approach that goes beyond mere wage increases. Businesses should actively engage with their employees to understand their needs and values, thereby tailoring benefits and solutions that are genuinely impactful. Among the solutions discussed are:

- *Financial Empowerment:* This includes innovative approaches such as integrating tipping options in digital payments, considering 401(k) plans with company matches, offering equity ownership, and providing retention bonuses to reduce turnover.

- *Growth and Development Opportunities:* Invest in employees' futures through tuition reimbursement programs, certification opportunities, internal training, and promoting from within. You can also offer financial literacy programs to empower employees in managing their personal finances.

- *Health and Wellness Programs:* Recognizing the challenges hourly workers face in accessing healthcare and taking time off, businesses could offer health insurance, childcare support, gym membership discounts, and meals during shifts.

- *Diversity, Equity, and Inclusion (DEI) Efforts:* Addressing bias in the hiring process and promoting a diverse and inclusive workplace should be a key focus. Solutions include training managers on fair hiring practices, hiring a chief diversity officer, and supporting the LGBTQ+ community.

- *Company Culture Initiatives:* Foster a positive work environment through regular social events like happy hours, implementing effective employee recognition programs, and ensuring open lines of communication between management and staff.

- *Recruiting Solutions:* It's important to engage with potential employees through social media and create effective job postings. Utilize different platforms for targeted recruiting and crafting job descriptions that are inclusive and appealing.
- *Employee Selection Solutions:* Businesses should improve the interview process and incorporate preemployment assessments to evaluate candidates more effectively and fairly.

While each of these solutions could be universally beneficial, keep in mind they should be tailored to the specific needs of a company's workforce. If appropriately implemented, these initiatives can improve recruitment, retention, productivity, and profitability, ultimately benefiting employees and employers.

In the next chapter, we'll shift our focus to what the future of hourly work might look like based on current trends and innovations. We'll explore how evolving technologies, changing societal attitudes, and economic shifts are shaping the landscape of hourly employment. You'll also discover insights into how businesses can adapt to these changes, get ahead of the game, and position themselves for success in a rapidly evolving labor market, ensuring that the needs and well-being of hourly workers remain at the forefront of these developments.

First, though, let's take a look at some real-life examples of companies successfully empowering their hourly workers through various workplace initiatives. This section features stories from ten major brands that found success with new programs, perks, or policies benefiting employees and the entire organization. You can review the results of their efforts and learn how to drive similar change within your own business, accelerating our progress toward a brighter future of work that we'll talk about in Chapter 5.

DELAWARE NORTH

No. of Hourly Workers Employed: 40,000
Industry: Global Hospitality and Entertainment Company
Perk/Policy Introduced: Culinary and Hospitality Excellence for Future Success (CHEFS®)
Date Introduced: May 2022

Reason Introduced:

The sudden outbreak of COVID-19 in 2020 severely disrupted the global hospitality industry. Even as Delaware North reopened in late 2020, pandemic layoffs, furloughs, and closures continued to impact hiring trends and the attitudes of culinary workers. In 2021, the company hired 1,700 culinarians but was unable to fill all the company's culinary needs. Faced with ongoing complexities — culinarian burnout, a diminishing culinary workforce, and high tuition rates curtailing culinary school enrollment — Delaware North took the opportunity to reimagine the talent and career development of its culinarians and created CHEFS®: a first-of-its-kind talent incubator for the company's culinarians.

Results/Impact:

CHEFS® established a premier culinary career progression program and culinary community that focuses on the culinary skills, social-emotional competency, and managerial development of the next generation of Delaware North's Cooks and Chefs. The structured 12-month on-the-job learning, mentoring, and training program, supported and led jointly by the Delaware North Culinary and Talent teams, and developed in collaboration with CIA Consulting, a division of the Culinary Institute of America (CIA), has offered hourly cooks and new Sous Chefs (Emerging Culinarians) rapid upward career progression. Emerging Culinarians are guided and mentored by Executive Chef Mentors, specially trained to nurture Emerging Culinarians in their technical and leadership culinary capability development.

Since May 2022, a combined 86 Chef Mentors and Emerging Culinarians have participated in CHEFS® with the goal for the latter of earning CIA ProChef® I and CIA ProChef® Baking and Pastry certifications, along with exclusive culinary-related promotions within Delaware North. Delaware North has also used this program to establish a benchmark of culinary and leadership capabilities for graduates. The company reports seeing growth in the confidence and the refinement of technical abilities at both the Executive Chef Mentor and Emerging Culinarian program levels.

SWEETGREEN

No. of Hourly Workers Employed: 5,000+
Industry: Food
Perk/Policy Introduced: Free meals for all Sweetgreen Team Members
(a.k.a. "Free Greens")
Date Introduced: ~2010

Reason Introduced:
Sweetgreen is on a mission to connect more communities to real food. This starts with the community of team members who bring our mission to life every day in our restaurants. Fueling our customer-facing teams with the healthy meals that we serve builds a fleet of natural brand advocates who can engage customers authentically with firsthand experience. It's a natural flywheel for our brand.

Results/Impact:
Through employee engagement surveys, we've found that eating at Sweetgreen correlates to higher team member engagement. Employees who regularly eat at Sweetgreen are happier at work and are more likely to keep working at Sweetgreen. Notably, team members who eat Sweetgreen during every shift or most shifts reported the highest level of satisfaction.

Additionally, employees have provided us with valuable feedback on our menu, most notably in 2016. It was a team member who introduced the idea of warm, grain-based bowls, which is now our most popular menu category.

We're proud of the impact that our commitment to the team member experience has had across our fleet. In 2023, turnover declined by over twenty points.

LUIHN VANTEDGE PARTNERS

No. of Hourly Workers Employed: 4,000
Industry: QSR
Perk/Policy Introduced: Employee Referral Program
Date Introduced: May 2021

Reason Introduced:

In May 2021, Luihn VantEdge Partners introduced an innovative Employee Referral Program aimed at tapping into the networks of its existing workforce. Employing 4,000 hourly workers across two hundred Taco Bell and KFC locations, the company aimed to utilize the personal connections of its employees to broaden its talent pool.

The Employee Referral Program at Luihn VantEdge Partners was crafted to inspire employees to share the exciting growth opportunities available at Taco Bell and KFC with their friends and family. This initiative not only sought to streamline the recruitment process but also aimed to cultivate a more connected and engaged workforce.

Results/Impact:

Since its inception, the Employee Referral Program has proven to be a success. In 2023 alone, the program paid out over $16,000 in employee referral bonuses, highlighting its efficacy in attracting high-quality candidates through the recommendations of current employees.

The impact of the Employee Referral Program extends beyond monetary incentives. By encouraging staff members to actively participate in the recruitment process, the company has fostered a sense of camaraderie and loyalty among its workforce.

Luihn VantEdge Partners' Employee Referral Program stands as a testament to the power of leveraging internal networks for recruitment within the QSR industry. This program not only streamlined the hiring process but also strengthened the bonds within the company's workforce. Positioned as a forward-thinking initiative, the Employee Referral Program at Luihn VantEdge Partners continues to propel success and innovation in the dynamic landscape of the fast-food industry.

THE SPINX COMPANY

No. of Hourly Workers Employed: 1,607
Industry: Retail Convenience Store
Perk/Policy Introduced: 401(k) Retirement Plan with Profit-Sharing
Date Introduced: 2000

Reason Introduced:

As founder of the Spinx Company, Stewart Spinks aimed to create a dynamic and diverse environment where team members could maximize their potential, secure a sustainable living, and plan for their retirement.

Results/Impact:

When Stewart Spinks created the Spinx Company, he truly wanted to make life easier with a commitment to fostering a positive workplace culture and providing all employees with opportunities for personal and financial growth. With that foundation in place, Spinx offers eligible hourly teammates a 401(k) retirement plan with profit-sharing to help teammates put themselves in a solid financial position for retirement. To help team members reach their retirement goals, Spinx matches their contributions from 1 to 6 percent of their pay for each dollar contributed. We are excited to have nearly 1,000 hourly teammates participating in our retirement/profit-sharing plan.

At Spinx, we understand that personal economic challenges can arise. As a result, we give teammates the option of taking a loan from their retirement account while continuing to contribute and make repayments on their loan through payroll. Since introducing the plan, we have increased our contribution yearly and seen the number of hourly teammates participating climb. While it took many years to grow the business financially, Stewart remains committed to fostering a positive workplace culture and providing employees with opportunities for personal and economic growth.

PAPA JOHNS

No. of Hourly Workers Employed: ~9,000

Industry: Pizza

Perk/Policy Introduced: Dough & Degrees tuition benefit program

Date Introduced: February 2019

Reason Introduced:

We introduced this to equip our team members to build fulfilling careers—whether at Papa Johns or elsewhere.

Results/Impact:

Dough & Degrees gives Papa Johns team members the opportunity to attend college and earn their degree at absolutely no cost to them. Papa Johns covers tuition, books, and fees—all paid for up front by Papa Johns, so there are no out-of-pocket expenses to team members. Team members can get high school diplomas, earn college credit for on-the-job training, get various degrees from associate's to master's, take professional certificate courses in business-relevant areas, and gain access to academic advising and guidance from learning experts.

As of December 2023, 600 team members have enrolled in Dough & Degrees, and 110 have earned a high school diploma, college degree, or a continuing professional education certificate. More than 80 percent of Dough & Degrees students are working on the front line in Papa Johns restaurants. Seventy-eight percent of graduates remain employed with Papa Johns, and many Dough & Degrees graduates are now applying their education in new roles across Papa Johns in departments such as Operations Excellence, Marketing, and Supply Chain. Corporate team members who average ten or more hours per week and are employed for at least two months at any Papa Johns–owned restaurant, quality control center, or corporate campus are eligible. Beginning in 2024, Papa Johns franchisees can elect to offer Dough & Degrees to their team members.

SIZZLING PLATTER

No. of Hourly Workers Employed: 15,000
Industry: Restaurant/Food Service
Perk/Policy Introduced: President's Club
Date Introduced: January 2023

Reason Introduced:

We introduced this to celebrate outstanding team member contributions to company culture and business performance to become an employer of choice.

Results/Impact:

The President's Club designation is awarded based on the improvement and maintenance of high employee sentiment (measured by daily surveys), reduction in employee turnover, achievement of training initiatives, team member promotions, and financial performance. It has introduced healthy competition and camaraderie among General Managers. Plus, it has significantly improved the company culture and financial performance of numerous restaurants. With so many GMs focused on these key initiatives, their efforts elevated company performance significantly across these metrics.

PANDA RESTAURANT GROUP, INC.

No. of Hourly Workers Employed: 43,465

Industry: Restaurant

Perk/Policy Introduced: Panda pays associates at least $1.00 above statutory requirements, even in locations with a $20/hr. minimum wage.

Date Introduced: 2024

Reason Introduced:

It has always been our philosophy to pay more than statutory requirements. Panda has been paying at least $0.50 more than statutory requirements for over 20 years.

Results/Impact:

Panda invests in associates by offering best-in-class competitive base pay. We not only benchmark ourselves to our fast-casual peers, but also to the living wage index. About 94% of our hourly associates earn at least $2.00/hour more than the statutory minimum wage.

Competitive compensation is both a widely mentioned perk from candidates and associates as well as a contributing factor to Panda being in the top quartile for restaurant industry turnover. Panda received the Best Practices Award by Black Box Intelligence for two consecutive years in 2023 and 2024 as one of the top-performing restaurants across various categories, including employee retention.

According to our 2023 company-wide engagement survey, over 75% of hourly associates rated favorably toward being paid fairly for their work. This is almost 10% above the Top 10% global benchmark and over 20% above the Restaurant & Hospitality industry benchmark.

ARBY'S

No. of Hourly Workers Employed: ~68,000
Industry: QSR
Perk/Policy Introduced: Igniting Dreams
Date Introduced: 2021

Reason Introduced:

Igniting Dreams is a grant program for Inspire Brands restaurant team members to help overcome barriers to personal growth and success. Potential recipients are encouraged to apply with the help of restaurant operations and field leaders. If awarded a grant, each recipient is given a sponsor to provide ongoing coaching, and team members can use the grant to overcome personal growth barriers such as textbooks, laptop purchases, vehicle deposits, and more.

Results/Impact:

In 2023, Igniting Dreams awarded 147 grants valued at $1,000, empowering individuals to overcome obstacles hindering their progress. Eighty-five of these applicants were also paired with mentors, fostering invaluable support and guidance. A noteworthy success story highlights the program's transformative impact:

Sydney Everett, who has been at Arby's for three years, dreams of advancing to shift manager. The grant will facilitate her goal by enabling her to secure a car, removing the transportation barrier hindering her promotion. With this step, Sydney can access higher education and fulfill her aspirations.

Through inspiring narratives and tangible outcomes like these, Igniting Dreams showcases the profound impact of investing in hourly workers. As we reflect on its success, let us champion similar initiatives within our organizations, ushering in a future where every team member's dreams are nurtured, and every aspiration is within reach.

BUFFALO WILD WINGS

No. of Hourly Workers Employed: ~65,000

Industry: QSR

Perk/Policy Introduced: Business Resource Groups

Date Introduced: February 2020

Reason Introduced:

Inspire's Business Resource Groups (BRGs) exemplify the company's commitment to diversity, inclusion, and employee development. Led by team members themselves, these groups serve as invaluable platforms for networking, leadership development, and mutual support.

Results/Impact:

From Black Voices at Inspire to Pride, each BRG plays a vital role in fostering a culture of empowerment and belonging:

- Black Voices at Inspire offers development opportunities and mentorship initiatives to support the advancement of black professionals within the organization, ensuring their voices are heard and valued.
- Champions of Women Leaders strengthens leadership skills and provides resources tailored to the needs of women in the workplace, empowering them to excel in their careers.
- Inspírate celebrates cultural diversity and promotes professional development within the Latino/Hispanic community, creating a nurturing environment where individuals can thrive.
- Inspire P2 fosters a community dedicated to personal and professional growth, fostering collaboration and knowledge-sharing among team members.
- Inspired Vets supports veterans and their families, offering resources and networking opportunities to facilitate their transition into civilian life and thrive in their careers.
- Pride provides a safe and inclusive space for LGBTQ+ team members and allies, promoting diversity of thought and ideas while fostering a culture of acceptance and respect.

Through these BRGs, Inspire cultivates a more inclusive workplace and empowers its employees to reach their full potential. By championing diversity and providing avenues for growth and support, Inspire sets a precedent for fostering a culture of excellence and belonging in the corporate world.

SONIC

No. of Hourly Workers Employed: ~85,128
Industry: QSR
Perk/Policy Introduced: Charity
Date Introduced: November 2020

Reason Introduced:

Sonic sparks brighter futures for America's youth by building strong communities where kids can thrive emotionally, mentally, and physically.

Results/Impact:

In the heart of Sonic Foundation lies a deep commitment to nurturing two fundamental pillars: Education and Community. Through our Limeades for Learning program, we invite guests to sip while students thrive. We understand that education is not confined to classroom walls; it's the guiding force that unlocks a child's boundless potential.

Similarly, we recognize the pivotal role of vibrant local communities in shaping promising futures. That's why we stand hand in hand with our operators, suppliers, franchisees, and grantees, investing in causes close to their hearts and the communities they serve. Our dedication yields impactful programs:

- SONIC Cares: In 2022, we proudly donated $3.4 million to support local classrooms, fostering environments where students can thrive.
- Limeades for Learning: With every sip, a portion of proceeds from Drink, Slush, and Shake purchases enriches the SONIC Foundation, empowering local public education initiatives.
- Sonic Disaster Relief: Upholding our belief in the power of relationships, our SONIC Disaster Relief Fund stands ready to support team members through life's toughest challenges.
- Sonic Swag Shop: Your purchases at our Swag Shop not only reflect your Sonic pride but also contribute to funding vital SONIC Foundation initiatives, directly impacting the communities our team members call home.

CHAPTER 5

The Future
of Work

Despite the oversaturation of negative headlines about AI and some uncertainties surrounding the introduction of Gen Z into the workforce, one thing is for certain: the future is bright but charged with tremendous change. Let's break it down based on trends we're seeing now, how they'll continue impacting the labor market, and what businesses can do to prepare today.

The Generation That Will Power It (Gen Z)

Lazy. Entitled. Impatient. Tech-addicted. Apathetic. The list of negative stereotypes about Generation Z goes on and on. But just like every generation before them, and likely all that come after, they will not be defined by presumptuous labels like these. Gen Zers are flooding into the workforce en masse, and this group has the potential to shape the future of work as we know it—in a good way.

There's disagreement on the precise years, but generally speaking, anyone born between the mid-1990s and early 2000s is a member of Gen Z. (Pew Research Center's range of 1995–2012 is a commonly used definition.[59]) Some of the oldest members of this generation would have graduated from college in 2020. So, in case you didn't know, Gen Z is already a big part of the workforce today. And as the largest generation to date, it is going to play an even bigger role in the workforce in the years to come.

There will be an estimated sixty-one million new job seekers entering the market from Gen Z, in total, including those who are already helping power our economy.[60] Of course, many of them will seek entry-level positions in the hourly workforce for their first jobs. Business owners and managers have already been scrambling to figure out this new generation of workers and how to effectively recruit and retain them. If you don't believe me, do a quick Google search. The sheer volume of articles on tips for managing the influx of Gen Zers in the workforce is astonishing.

So, is there any truth to the labels and stereotypes some people have assigned to Gen Z? What will the largest and most ethnically diverse generation actually bring to the table? How will their unique values change the way we treat employees, especially those in the hourly workforce?

59   Insider Intelligence, "Generation Z: Facts," accessed February 7, 2024, https://www.insiderintelligence.com/insights/generation-z-facts/.

60   Concordia University, St. Paul, "Generation Z in the Workforce," accessed February 7, 2024, https://online.csp.edu/resources/infographic/generation-z-in-the-workforce/.

Ambitious. Hardworking. Eager. Tech-savvy. Value-driven. These are likely far more accurate labels in describing the majority of Gen Zers than the negative ones you've heard. And just like with any generation, they have their own story and background that shape their strengths and weaknesses in society. For business owners and managers, it's all about playing to those strengths and coaching them through their weaknesses.

However, it's clear this generation will not simply accept the status quo and be told how things are going to be at work. They're champions of innovation and crave purposeful work. They've seen their parents struggle financially, likely contributing to their frugal nature and desire to save early for retirement. They've also been hyper-connected to social media and digital platforms with content about poor working conditions and employee mistreatment at companies across the country. (That's right, it's not just scrolling through pictures of cute dogs or watching makeup tutorials. Social media is where Gen Zers get news updates from major media outlets as well.)

Ultimately, whether you're ready to admit it or not, we're at a point where job seekers will dictate what the future of work looks like. And the changes have already begun.

Mobile-First Everything

One of the most evident trends happening right now is the shift to a mobile-first approach to virtually every aspect of the hiring process. If you haven't noticed, look up. You might be living under a rock… Kidding aside, research shows that 91 percent of Americans keep their cell phones within arm's reach at all times. *All times.* How many other items can we say that about aside from clothes?

Ready for another surprising stat? Ninety percent of all text messages are read within three minutes of being sent.[61] You can't say that about emails, which typically have an open rate between 20 and 40 percent. Here's another one: text messages are opened and read almost 138 percent more than email.[62]

OK, I think you get the picture. All of these stats paint a pretty clear picture of what businesses must do to keep up with the labor market moving forward: Make literally everything mobile-friendly. Or, at least, as much as you can. Applicant tracking systems and other HR tech providers have started to adapt with features like text-to-apply. There are several other areas you can work on, though.

Think about the journey of a job seeker today. Step one usually involves visiting a job board website. The job board should have you covered by making their website or app mobile-friendly, but what about your job description? Make sure it's not unnecessarily long, forcing users to scroll endlessly to find important information about the opportunity. Most people only spend a few seconds reading job posts and give it a quick glance before swiping to the next advertisement. Keep it short and sweet, and put the most important information near the top. (When I say "most important," I mean what would be most important to Gen Z job seekers who want to know about salary, benefits, and workplace culture.)

Now, if someone hears that your company is hiring, whether from an ad or word of mouth from a friend, they'll likely visit your website and immediately click on your careers page. Think it's just one

---

61 VentureBeat, "Why Businesses Can't Ignore SMS: Hint: 90% of People Read a Text Message within the First 3 Minutes," accessed February 7, 2024, https://venturebeat.com/business/why-businesses-cant-ignore-sms-hint-90-of-people-read-a-text-message-within-the-first-3-minutes/.

62 Statflo, "Best Practices for Business Text Messaging," accessed February 7, 2024, https://www.statflo.com/blog/best-practices-business-text-messaging.

of those "must-haves" that every company website has and it's all right if it doesn't look great? Think again. Your careers page could be the first impression a potentially great hire has of your business, and we all know how crucial first impressions are. Make it enticing. Highlight your company's values. Its story. Highlight who *you* are.

Feature your team with a snippet about each of them to show you actually care about your employees. Remember, Gen Z job seekers want purposeful work and have ambitions for meaningful growth. Show them what you stand for and that working for your company isn't just another dead-end job. (By the way, it doesn't hurt to throw a little SEO on your careers page. In case you don't know, that means enriching it with certain keywords and phrases your ideal applicants are likely to enter into a search engine like Google.)

The next step in the job seeker journey is an interesting one, not because completing it is particularly interesting—because it's actually quite the opposite—but because there seems to be a lot of disconnect between employers and candidates at this stage. It's the application itself. Let me start by asking if you'd like to fill out an application with fifty-plus repetitive questions and manually input every detail from your résumé after you've *already* uploaded your résumé and attached it to your application. Do you have time for that? Probably not, and neither do your potential hires. They're likely just as busy as you and shouldn't have to go through such a tedious process when they're thinking there's a good chance you'll reject them or never even view their application.

Now, we have the interview stage, assuming an applicant has made it this far. As with everything else, make sure this step is mobile-friendly as well. Consider giving candidates the option of virtual interviews instead of making them come in for an in-person discussion. It can still be "face-to-face" with the help of video interviewing software these days. Plus, you might otherwise limit your applicant pool since a lot of potentially great hires might not have easy access to transportation or have trouble coordinating times, especially if they're working another job.

If you are hesitant to make a hiring decision without a candidate physically coming in for an interview, that's fair. However, it may be an obstacle you'll have to move past if current trends[63] continue with the rise of video interviews, one-way interviews with applicants recording responses to preset questions, AI-based interviews, and even companies not requiring interviews at all. As a Gen Z job seeker, would you want to have an in-person interview at a business that might not even hire you or enjoy the convenience of a virtual interview? One manager gets ghosted in this scenario, and the other gets a potentially great hire.

Finally, there's the onboarding paperwork. This should be an easy one with all the tools that can securely send paperwork and collect electronic signatures. Nobody wants to spend their first day of work reading through stacks of papers with HR. This should all be done conveniently via a phone or tablet prior to their first day so they can hit the ground running, benefiting you both.

---

63   Forbes Business Council, "The Virtual Interview Is the New Resume: What You Need to Know," accessed February 7, 2024, https://www.forbes.com/sites/forbesbusinesscouncil/2022/05/05/the-virtual-interview-is-the-new-resume-what-you-need-to-know/?sh=5f816625486d.

Everything Will Be Faster

Remember the study[64] my company and I conducted that found 50 percent of applicants surveyed expect to hear from managers within three days, and 11 percent want to hear within twenty-four hours? Well, there are plenty more like it, including one that found 40 percent of candidates rejected a job offer because they accepted another one before the other company even finished the hiring process.[65]

And that research was conducted over ten years ago! Can you imagine what that stat would look like today with Gen Z? The old saying, "speed is of the essence," will be truer than ever moving forward. A fast hiring process will be of the utmost importance for businesses to stay competitive in securing top talent. It's not just about securing the best workers, though. The faster your hiring process, the faster you can fill open positions, alleviating the pressure on workers who are forced to pick up the slack and likely nearing the point of burnout.

You can speed up your hiring process by making it mobile-friendly with the tips above, especially by simplifying applications and communicating with applicants and employees via text message. However, there are further steps that will help you improve the candidate experience, fill open positions faster, and lighten the workload on hiring managers.

Brace yourself if you're opposed to tech because the future of work will likely have a lot of it, and these solutions are no exception. This

---

64   Forbes Human Resources Council, "Candidate Ghosting: New Insight into Today's Hiring Epidemic," accessed February 7, 2024, https://www.forbes.com/sites/forbeshumanresourcescouncil/2023/09/05/candidate-ghosting-new-insight-into-todays-hiring-epidemic/?sh=2edb6ae72f48.

65   Fox Business, "Want to Hire the Best Candidate? Move Fast," accessed February 7, 2024, https://www.foxbusiness.com/features/want-to-hire-the-best-candidate-move-fast.

trend isn't going anywhere anytime soon, and solutions can automate and reduce time spent on tedious tasks that nobody wants to do anyway. There are tools that are becoming more and more effective at virtually every step of the hiring process, from recruiting applicants to screening candidates and guiding new hires through the onboarding process.

I'll use my company's software, for example. The Sprockets platform includes an AI-powered virtual recruiter that sources, screens, and schedules interviews with applicants in a way that feels authentic and conversational. Rather than traditional chatbots that use rule-based algorithms (i.e., if they ask this, respond with that), "JoJo" adapts to any situation with personalized, engaging responses and ensures a smooth hiring process. Of course, she uses text messages as the preferred method of communication for Gen Z and the new generation of hourly workers.

Basically, the entire hiring process can be completed via a text message conversation while our Applicant Matching System simultaneously determines whether the applicants will succeed and stay long term, then alerts managers about top candidates. There's no need to replace anything unless you want to since JoJo can essentially be your own hiring manager who works 24/7/365. Managers can focus on daily operations and simply have interviews automatically added to their calendars with the ideal candidates for open positions. She even automatically reaches out to applicants you may not have contacted or hired in the past but may need them now when she's notified you have a new opening.

Essentially, JoJo creates a constantly growing community of readyto-work candidates to automatically fill positions in minutes, not days or months. No more struggling to cover shifts and dealing with a time-intensive hiring process. At the very least, the automated recruiting and matching based on key personality traits allows managers to start on the twenty-yard-line when they go to interview applicants since they know they're a good fit, rather than starting on their own goal line and knowing the bare minimum that's on résumés. Again, it's a win-win for applicants and employers alike.

This is not meant to be a plug for my company. It's simply an example that, naturally, I know more about than other solutions on the market. But I think you get the point. Automated tools like JoJo significantly accelerate the entire hiring process by automating tedious tasks, enabling managers to focus on other important operations that contribute to the success of the business.

Community-Based Workplaces

I mentioned creating a community of applicants using Sprockets and JoJo to maintain communication with potential hires, but Gen Zers will likely want to feel like their workplace is a community as well. Business owners and managers shouldn't "let off the gas" when it comes to engagement after someone is hired. It's crucial to establish a positive environment, identify which candidates will contribute to that positivity, and continue engagement initiatives posthire. Generation Z craves the opportunity to grow and hone skills.

As much as some might say they are entitled, similar to what people said about millennials, Gen Zers are more than willing to work hard and earn their chances. However, owners and managers must create career paths and help foster their growth through mentorship programs and ongoing training.

Looking forward, it should be a community of diverse, hard-working professionals all working together and "cheering each other on" to constantly better themselves, in a sense. It starts with company culture and continues with efforts from management to make every day feel like a team effort to grow the business as well as each other's skills. Then, it continues by giving hourly workers the opportunity to prove they can move up the ladder and take on extra responsibilities.

Call me a broken record, but it really is a win-win when you create a workplace that feels like a community of growth, inclusivity, and opportunity. You'll likely see an improvement in employee retention, positive results from internal promotions, and an increase in applicant flow from reputation as well as referrals from current employees.

Better Benefits and Flexibility

The trifecta of Gen Z's financial concerns, competition in the labor market, and the rise of tech means that there will likely be a nationwide shift toward better benefits packages for employees. As we discussed earlier, this generation has seen their parents struggle financially, wants to start saving for retirement earlier than past generations, and craves purposeful work with opportunities for growth. The competition among understaffed businesses and the sheer volume of Gen Zers in the hourly workforce gives them the leverage to ask for such things. And tech-enabled solutions make it easier than ever to provide workers with different types of benefits.

Chipotle's chief human resources officer, Ilene Eskenazi, recently stated, "As we push toward our long-term goal of operating 7,000 restaurants in North America, it's crucial that we listen to and adapt to the needs of our team members, so they can grow with us."[66] She goes on to say that Gen Z "faces notable financial challenges" that they've announced new benefits to help with. That's not all. Gen Z already

---

66   QSR Magazine, "Chipotle Unveils New Benefits Aimed at Gen Z Workforce," accessed February 6, 2024, https://www.qsrmagazine.com/story/chipotle-unveils-new-benefits-aimed-at-gen-z-workforce/.

makes up 73 percent of Chipotle's current workforce, and Eskenazi says, "Empowering our talent is embedded in our company's culture."

Their new offerings include a variety of benefits to improve their workers' financial and mental health, including a Student Loan Retirement Match program that helps them pay off student loans while saving for retirement. In the realm of tech-enabled benefit solutions, they've also announced employees will be able to use Cred.ai's "Credit Optimizer" tool and an extensive EAP. It doesn't stop there. Chipotle has long been a prime example of a brand that invests in the growth of its employees with internal promotions. Ninety percent of their workers in leadership roles once started out as crew members. The list goes on. What Chipotle has done in recent years and what the company continues to do is commendable and shows they know what drives the new generation of workers.

Is your company taking a serious look at how your benefits programs can adapt to attract and retain new workers? If not, now's the time. Traditional benefits won't cut it anymore, and they really didn't cut it before either.

Increase in Gig Culture

One of the most sought-after benefits is a flexible schedule, which enables workers to achieve a healthy work-life balance as well as pick up side gigs for extra money. Commonly referred to simply as the "gig economy,"[67] these short-term contract and freelance roles give people a chance to compensate for low pay at their regular jobs and even pick up new skills. These types of opportunities could even help people get by after being laid off from their full-time jobs.

---

67   Omnes Group, "Gen Z and the Gig Economy," accessed February 6, 2024, https://www.omnesgroup.com/gen-z-and-the-gig-economy/.

They could be driving for rideshare services, delivering groceries, selling handmade crafts, and so much more. Tech is at the core of a lot of gig opportunities, with platforms like Uber and Etsy making it easier than ever to get started. Expect more of these to be introduced to the market, and prepare for the likelihood your hourly workers will desire a flexible schedule so they can supplement their cash flow with gig jobs, among other reasons.

No Résumés or Cover Letters

I've heard people toss the idea around for a while now about removing résumés and cover letters from the hiring process, but I don't think many of them thought such drastic changes would actually happen. Recent research indicates Gen Zers might advocate for them, though. A study found that one in three Gen Zers want to remove résumés from the application process, and four in five Gen Zers want to remove cover letters. Let's ponder this for a bit.

Résumés have been used to evaluate job applicants for so long that it might be tough to imagine a hiring process without them. Do they really tell the whole story of a person, though? A single piece of paper cannot sufficiently describe someone's experience, personality, and potential. While résumés can still help you quickly find candidates with the right technical skills, they shouldn't be the sole focus of your search.

Anyone who has written a résumé is familiar with the headaches involved in finding the right layout, creating several drafts to perfect the language, and constantly updating it with new information. (Résumé writing services are popular for a reason!) However, is it worth all the time and effort people put into them?

The average recruiter only spends six to seven seconds reviewing a résumé.[68] These hasty decisions often lead to first-impression bias, the leading cause of hiring errors.[69] Unfortunately, that means many résumés are ignored or thrown away simply because of the name at the top. One study even showed that minority applicants who changed certain details of their résumés to make them seem more "white" received more interviews.[70] It doesn't have to be this way.

So, where do we go from here? One popular option is to use LinkedIn as "resumes." In fact, 87 percent of recruiters find LinkedIn most effective when looking for potential hires.[71] These profiles contain a lot of key information about candidates, they're easily skimmable, and employers can filter potential hires based on certain keywords, like workplace skills or job titles. Plus, Generation Z is no stranger to social media platforms like LinkedIn. The future of work will also see an uptick in the use of preemployment assessments, mentioned earlier, which numerous companies have already started using. They have the potential to eliminate the need for résumés altogether.

As for cover letters, I can see them being eliminated from the hiring process as well. They are time-consuming for both applicants and employers. Is it realistic to ask hiring managers to read every

---

68 Indeed, "How Long Do Employers Look at Resumes?," accessed February 6, 2024, https://www.indeed.com/career-advice/resumes-cover-letters/how-long-do-employers-look-at-resumes.

69 LinkedIn Talent Solutions, "Eliminate First Impression Bias and Hire the Right Candidate," accessed February 6, 2024, https://www.linkedin.com/business/talent/blog/talent-strategy/eliminate-first-impression-bias-and-hire-right-candidate.

70 Harvard Business School Working Knowledge, "Minorities Who 'Whiten' Job Resumes Get More Interviews," accessed February 6, 2024, https://hbswk.hbs.edu/item/minorities-who-whiten-job-resumes-get-more-interviews.

71 Fast Company, "This Is What Recruiters Look for on Your LinkedIn Profile," accessed February 6, 2024, https://www.fastcompany.com/3067594/this-is-what-recruiters-look-for-on-your-linkedin-profile.

single applicant's cover letter, especially when click-to-apply culture has already made it virtually impossible for humans to properly review all applications? They may still find their place in the white-collar, salaried workforce, especially as a way for experienced professionals to expand upon their lengthy CVs. However, I can't see them lasting long in the hourly workforce.

Have No Fear, AI Is Here (Seriously)

I've seen more headlines than I can count in the last couple of years about the "rise of AI" and how it's going to dramatically change nearly everything in our lives. Heck, I woke up to dozens of newsletters like that in my inbox this morning, and I'm sure I've gotten at least a few more while writing this paragraph. Will I read them all? Not likely. Sure, some of the recent content out there on AI has value. But as someone who is very familiar with the topic and has built a company from the ground up providing AI-powered hiring software to businesses, I have to say it feels like a lot of it has been sensationalized.

There are too many articles lately that seem to take advantage of the public's misplaced fear of artificial intelligence. I say "misplaced" because we shouldn't be afraid of AI or the idea of integrating it into the hiring process. AI isn't anything new. It's been around for years and has already taken its place in so many aspects of society to improve our daily lives. You just might not realize it.

Think you haven't used artificial intelligence today? Let's run through a few quick questions. Did you use FaceID to unlock your phone? AI. Have you checked out your personalized feed on social media? AI. Have you asked Siri a question? AI. Did an app help you avoid traffic on your way to work? AI.

I could go on and on, but that would make for a boring book, even though I'm sure I could fill at least a few pages with examples. The point is you're already using AI, and it makes daily tasks so much easier that could otherwise be frustrating and time-consuming. It sure sounds like a solution that could help with tasks in the hiring process that are frustrating and time-consuming. Those who don't adopt it, or wait too long to adopt it, will be at a disadvantage in the future labor market. They're already at a disadvantage compared to all the companies that have implemented AI-powered tools. Skynet won't infiltrate your system anytime soon, and you don't have to worry about Arnold Schwarzenegger breaking through walls in your office. (Although, wouldn't that be pretty cool?)

It's also interesting to note that, somewhat paradoxically, allowing tech to take over some human-driven tasks in the hiring process can actually help *humanize* the hourly workforce by removing bias from the equation.

Of course, I know that AI-powered tools and new tech solutions have replaced jobs and tasks historically performed by humans. We've already seen grocery stores set up self-checkout lanes, fast-food restaurants use voice AI in drive-thru lanes, and airports use kiosks for passengers to get their plane tickets. And don't forget about ATMs, which debuted in the United States in 1969.[72] Ultimately, customer-facing roles have been the first to go, and this will likely be the case moving forward as well. Is it a bad thing? Maybe. Maybe not. This trend opens up possibilities for streamlining business operations, improving customer experiences, and freeing up actual employees for other important tasks. Rather than seeing millions of people lose their jobs entirely like some headlines might have you believe, I think

---

72 History.com, "First ATM Opens for Business," accessed February 6, 2024, https://www.history.com/this-day-in-history/first-atm-opens-for-business.

there will be a shift in the priority of tasks performed by the hourly workforce. There will always be a need for workers.

How Tech Can Drive the Future of the Hiring Process

Remember the story of Marco in chapter 1, with all the challenges he faced and hoops he had to jump through to secure a job? That's what millions of people in the hourly workforce must deal with on a regular basis. But AI and automation make the possibilities almost limitless for the future of the hiring process.

So, if we could imagine the ideal hiring process, what would it look like? In an ideal world, it would be a frictionless process that treats each applicant with dignity rather than them feeling like "just another number" in a company's applicant tracking system. I'm not forgetting about the hiring managers either. The hiring process has historically failed them, as well, putting unrealistic expectations and pressure on them to screen, select, and engage with a high volume of applicants.

Back to step one of the applicant journey. Rather than blindly searching for jobs based on keywords you think you'd be a good fit for, wouldn't it be great if a system could send you instant alerts about open positions you're *guaranteed* to be a great fit for and check off all the boxes for your ideal job?

Then, rather than submitting a lengthy application with pretty much the same exact questions as every other company hiring hourly workers, a system keeps your profile on record to automatically submit with the click of a button when you get an alert on your phone. Oh yeah, your résumé would also be saved, so you don't have to keep entering it manually despite submitting it separately as an attachment on every single application.

Now for the interview stage. It doesn't exist. Or, at least, it doesn't exist in the way we know it today. People would be matched to jobs, and managers would also get alerts when their ideal candidate is found in the system. They could schedule an interview if they really want to, but the system would be reliable and consistent enough that managers could send a job offer with a click of a button on their phones—trusting the matching system to do *its* job. It could even identify there's a job opening as soon as someone leaves, find a new match, and send alerts to managers so they're never really understaffed for more than a few minutes.

No bias. No time wasted. No inefficiencies. Just a hiring system that runs nonstop to match the ideal candidates to businesses that need them—even while they sleep. 24/7/365. No breaks for weekends, sick days, or vacations. It maintains a human-based approach to hiring, although somewhat paradoxically, by removing humans from the hiring process. Managers are freed up to focus on daily operations, improving customer satisfaction while contributing to the growth of the company, while employees enjoy waking up every morning for meaningful work at places that value them and feel more like communities than just companies.

Key Takeaways

I realize this might sound like an impossible goal, but I truly believe a brighter future is possible, even though it might not look exactly how I outlined it. We can make a real difference if we come together to shift our mindsets, invest in new solutions, and make conscious efforts to bridge the gap between employers and employees. Hourly workers can no longer go unseen. They can no longer be treated as transactional resources.

It's no longer all right to accept high turnover rates. They aren't just numbers. They are real human beings with real lives beyond their hourly jobs, and there are real consequences to how they are treated day to day in the workplace. Plus, every time an hourly worker is fired or quits, it hurts both them and the company. And on a large scale across the country, it hurts the economy and greater society. Remember, turnover is literally a trillion-dollar problem in the United States.[73]

> **Overlooking or mistreating a single hourly worker has consequences that ripple throughout society, but "seeing" them and treating them with respect and understanding can have equally impactful *positive effects* on society.**

I know we won't get there overnight, but progress is being made, and we can accelerate our journey toward that brighter future by taking the right steps—together. I mean, imagine a workplace where respect, understanding, and inclusion are all baked into the culture.

Employee engagement hits an all-time high, with everyone feeling as an actual part of a community that values each person's livelihood. Turnover rates hit an all-time low since workers enjoy coming to work every day. Customer satisfaction goes through the roof as they are indirect recipients of the positivity instilled in the workforce. Now, imagine that at every workplace in America. No, imagine it at just 50

---

73   Gallup, "A Fixable Problem That Costs Businesses $1 Trillion," accessed February 6, 2024, https://www.gallup.com/workplace/247391/fixable-problem-costs-businesses-trillion.aspx.

percent of them. It sounds idyllic, but it's attainable. I've seen glimpses of it, and I can't wait for the vision to become a reality for the entire hourly workforce.

Conclusion

In my position, I'm naturally asked if I'm optimistic or pessimistic about the direction of the hourly workforce. By investors. By customers. By prospects.

"Are things getting better?"

"How are things changing?"

In fact, my career is predicated on my ability to answer these questions. It's charged with scaling responsibility as the company grows and my personal influence flourishes. To investors. To my team. To hiring managers. To millions of hourly workers.

The truth is that it's a wildly complex question charged with incredibly complicated factors and ever-changing goalposts. It's hard to give a simple answer because it's charged with seemingly unlimited nuance and complications.

I like to answer this in two parts.

First, with a Timeline

My answer always starts with my favorite line: "When you're in the trenches, it's sometimes hard to see if you're winning the war." This is important for everyone to understand.

Those who are intimate with the hourly workforce understand that it's not always pretty. The invisible workforce is largely under-resourced, without opportunities, and hurting. Hiring managers don't have the right tools and oftentimes don't have the appetite to create overnight change. Financial markets don't reward companies and innovations within this sector to accelerate advancement.

We, as an industry and society, need to continue to focus on this group and have ten lifetimes worth of work to do. However, there's hope.

HR tech companies are working for change.

Hiring managers are working for change.

Policymakers are working for change.

Like most difficult problems, it can be helpful to force perspective and zoom out. How have we progressed in the past two years? Ten years? Twenty-five? One hundred? Have we created enough "dots" to create a positive trend "line" of progress?

The answer is clear: absolutely.

There is no shortage of challenges to solve in the hourly workforce, but it's important to know that we have made tremendous ground and won major battles in this war. Because of the hard work of millions of passionate people, we've seen a renaissance of legislation change over the past 150 years that has positively impacted hourly workers.

- 1913: Department of Labor
    - The United States Department of Labor was established on March 4, 1913. It was created as a result of the Department of Labor and Commerce Act, which split the Department of Commerce and Labor into two separate entities: the Department of Labor and the Department of Commerce. The Department of Labor's primary focus is

on labor-related issues, including workplace conditions, employment, and the welfare of workers.

- 1916: Workers Compensation
  - □ The Federal Employees' Compensation Act (FECA) was established in 1916, covering federal employees. These laws generally provide compensation and medical benefits to employees who suffer work-related injuries or illnesses, regardless of fault. The aim is to ensure financial protection for workers and streamline the process of obtaining compensation without the need for lengthy legal battles. Specific details can vary between states and federal jurisdictions.

- 1920: Women's Bureau
  - □ The Women's Bureau was created on June 5, 1920, as a result of the Women's Bureau Act signed into law by President Woodrow Wilson. Its primary purpose was to promote the welfare of working women and to advocate for their rights and interests in the labor force.
  - □ The Women's Bureau conducts research, gathers data, and provides information on various issues related to women in the workplace. Its focus includes matters such as working conditions, wages, and legislation affecting women workers. The establishment of the Women's Bureau marked a significant step in recognizing and addressing the specific concerns of women in the workforce during the early twentieth century.

- 1935: Social Security
  - □ The Social Security program in the United States was established with the passage of the Social Security Act on August 14, 1935, during the presidency of Franklin D. Roosevelt. The program was designed to provide economic security and assistance to individuals who are retired, unemployed, or disabled. Social Security is funded through payroll taxes and provides benefits such as retirement income, disability benefits, and survivor benefits to eligible individuals and their families.

- 1938: Child Labor Laws
  - □ The Fair Labor Standards Act (FLSA) of 1938, enacted in the United States, set national standards for minimum wage, overtime pay eligibility, recordkeeping, and child labor. This act established age restrictions and working hour limitations for minors, effectively outlawing oppressive child labor practices. However, the specifics and timing of child labor laws vary across countries, with many nations implementing similar measures in the twentieth century to protect the rights and well-being of young workers.

- 1963: Equal Pay Act
  - □ The Equal Pay Act of 1963 is a US federal law aimed at eliminating gender-based wage discrimination. It mandates that employers provide equal pay for equal work, regardless of gender, by prohibiting wage disparities between employees of different sexes who perform substantially similar jobs. The law promotes workplace

equality and aims to address the long-standing issue of gender-based wage gaps.

- 1964: Civil Rights Act
  - The Civil Rights Act of 1964 is a landmark US federal law that prohibits discrimination on the basis of race, color, religion, sex, or national origin. Title VII of this act specifically addresses employment practices. It aims to ensure equal employment opportunities and prohibits employers from discriminating against employees or job applicants based on the protected characteristics. The legislation marked a crucial step in promoting civil rights and combating discrimination in various aspects of American society, including the workplace.

- 1965: EEOC
  - The US Equal Employment Opportunity Commission (EEOC) was founded on July 2, 1965. It is a federal agency responsible for enforcing federal laws that prohibit employment discrimination based on race, color, religion, sex, national origin, age, disability, or genetic information. The EEOC investigates and resolves complaints of discrimination, works to prevent discrimination through education and outreach, and also provides guidance to employers and employees regarding their rights and responsibilities under antidiscrimination laws. The agency plays a crucial role in promoting equal employment opportunities and ensuring fairness in the workplace.

- 1978: Age Discrimination Laws
  - In 1978, the US Congress passed the Age Discrimination in Employment Act (ADEA). The ADEA is a federal law that prohibits discrimination against employees and job applicants who are forty years of age or older on the basis of age. It protects individuals from age-related discrimination in various aspects of employment, including hiring, promotions, job assignments, compensation, and terminations. The ADEA aims to promote the employment of older individuals based on their abilities and qualifications rather than age-related stereotypes.

- 1990: Americans with Disabilities Act (ADA)
  - The ADA prohibits discrimination against individuals with disabilities in various areas, including employment.

- 1993: Family and Medical Leave Act (FMLA)
  - FMLA allows eligible employees to take unpaid, job-protected leave for specified family and medical reasons, including the birth or adoption of a child and serious health conditions.

- 2010: Affordable Care Act (ACA)
  - The ACA includes provisions related to employer-sponsored health plans and the expansion of Medicaid, impacting aspects of employee benefits.

- 2020: Title VII of the Civil Rights Act
  - In a landmark decision in June 2020, the US Supreme Court ruled in Bostock v. Clayton County that discrimi-

nation based on sexual orientation and gender identity is a form of sex discrimination prohibited by Title VII of the Civil Rights Act of 1964. This decision provides federal workplace protections for LGBTQ+ employees.

When I review this timeline, I think to myself, "My children are entering a far better workforce than my great-grandparents."

To me, much of my optimism comes from the communal effort that's collectively lifted this space over the past few decades. For any major change to occur, especially in workforce development or management, several parties must collaborate. No single person, company, or technology can serve as a silver bullet. However, when we work together—lawmakers, technologists, employers, advocates—real progress can be made. It will never move fast enough, but progress is progress, and forced perspective shows a clear line up to the right over the past one hundred years.

Second, a Story

Growing up, starfish were sacred to us. From kitchen decor to beach towels, the five-armed figures filled my house. It's all based on a simple idea that my great-grandparents passed down from generation to generation. On beaches in the Northeast, every year, starfish wash up the shore en masse. It attracts beachgoers from all over the world.

The sad reality that's forgotten as people upload pictures to their Instagram is that every starfish pictured on that beach will die slowly from suffocation. If they are lucky, a bird will pick them up for a quicker death. This doesn't stop tourists from flocking to the area to take pictures, poke at the creatures, and even take them as souvenirs.

One morning, a small boy walks down the beach. An old man watches as he picks up a starfish up from the sand and throws it back into the ocean. He takes a few more steps and does the same thing. Finally, the old man approaches the boy and asks, "What are you doing?"

"I'm saving the starfish," the boy says.

Stunned. The old man looks around. There are tens of thousands scattered across the beach. He waves his hands to emphasize the scale of the problem. "You'll never save them," he shouts. "It's no use."

The boy smiles. He picks up another starfish at the old man's feet and heaves it past the first wave line. "Well, I just saved that one." He throws another. "And that one." He throws one more. "And that one."

While the old man was stunned by the magnificent, unsolvable problem, the boy took action. He certainly didn't throw back every starfish that day, but he saved all that he could. And that matters.

I see the hourly workforce the same way.

Yes, this is a magnificent problem that no one person can solve, but every day, every person must choose to either walk by the starfish or throw them back into the ocean.

Every day, we have an opportunity to positively impact the hourly workforce.

I choose to throw back starfish. Will you?

For employers: This means seeing and investing in your people. It doesn't take a herculean effort to help hourly workers. Although we've outlined some programs that require sweeping changes, there are other things that you can do today to humanize the hourly workers. It's good for business, but it's also good for humanity.

For salaried workers: You do not need to be in HR or the C-suite to influence change. Approach your hourly peers. Walk down to the warehouse. Introduce yourself. Get to know the team. Listen to them. If you've enjoyed this book and feel it may be helpful to your employer, give it to your HR manager or CEO.

For the hourly worker: Keep faith. Hold your employers accountable to provide strong programming to help navigate your life. Know that although it's not light right now, the wheels of progress are rolling.

For those unemployed: See the hourly workers on your journey. Talk to the flight attendant. Pick up after yourselves in a hotel room. Stack the plates in a restaurant. Say please and thank you.

Whether you're the CEO of a Fortune 500, a manager at a small business, or just someone trying to make it to Friday, you can positively influence this invisible group.

If you've read this far, I'm hopeful that, above all, you've come to appreciate the importance of humanizing the hourly workforce. This group of people is worthy of respect from everyone. However, they are often misunderstood, underrepresented, and unseen.

So, the next time you notice someone servicing you, cleaning for you, caring for you, say "Hi" to Danny for me.